AUTHENTIC FAITH

Encountering the love of God, knowing Him, and your place through Christ

Israel Chukwuka Okunwaye

Author/Publisher, ©Israel Chukwuka Okunwaye 2018.

For all correspondence, address to–

> 27 Old Gloucester Street, London
> WC1N 3AX
> United Kingdom
> or, Email: write@israelokunwaye.com

Printed by *CreateSpace*, an Amazon.com Company. Available on Kindle and other retail outlets.

Israel Chukwuka Okunwaye has asserted all his rights under the Copyright, Designs and Patents Act, 1998, to be identified as Author of this work.

The Author/Publisher has used his best endeavours to ensure that the URLs for external websites referred to in this book are correct and active at the time of going to press. However, the Author/Publisher has no responsibility for the websites and can make no guarantee that a site will remain live or that the content will remain relevant, decent or appropriate.

Unless otherwise stated, Scripture quotations [from the specified version and passage references] in this publication are from the Holy Bible. All rights reserved.

First published 2018

British Library Cataloguing in Publication Data: a catalogue record for this book is available from the British Library.

ISBN: 978-1-9164445-1-5

www.israelokunwaye.com
www.glyglobal.com

To all in the humble journey of faith desiring to know God in a fresh and deeper way.

CONTENT

TITLE PAGE

DEDICATION

INTRODUCTION

PART I: THE GOD OF THE GOSPEL

PART II: THE GOSPEL OF JESUS CHRIST

PART III BE INSPIRED

INTRODUCTION

I wish to present to you my work on necessary spiritual belief. My hope is that it blesses you and that you come to realise more deeply the extent of God's love for you through faith. It will bless you, if you read through meticulously, ponder on it with an open mind and then receive it into your heart. I have taken diligent care to bring together some of my finest teachings and writings through the years [by the inspiration of the Spirit of God], on the person of God and what He has done in Jesus Christ of Nazareth; and how that inspires faith which is spiritually rich and true– that is authentic. I substantially rely on the bible to examine this matter of faith in Christ. I also do refer to some authors to buttress my point further, and to illustrate how divergent themes assist in making clearer this spiritual reality. The bible clearly presents Christ as the object of the Christian's affection and hope for a lost world, as the way to knowing Jehovah God, and for resolving any mind-boggling inquiry on humanity's future. I have been faithful to this gracious fundamental perspective, which is according to the bible and the testimony of those who trust Christ as messiah; that the Lord Jesus represents that which is a gift to all for salvation and the glorious eschatological hope for the believer. For someone in need of a honest understanding on what faith is, this book would be helpful for you. Freely I have received from the Lord, freely I give. I wrote each page of this book with the reader in mind, being willing to share each leaf a foretime of publishing, trusting each benevolent path would leave the hearer richer, and being also willing to research along the chosen lines to bring together a crafted piece that exudes emphasis on the magnificence of God, and the necessity of the quest for deeper intimacy with the one true divine.

So, I am sharing with you my labour of love through the years. I hope you become engrossed with this material at every level of its exposition, but above all that you find a wholesome and uncontradictory answer to the God question you are asking, through the revelation of Christ. God is not responsible for a conflicting opinion of His person, it is your obligation to search out what is true about Him– and the good story is, He has made that known already. Do you really want to know Him, and know what is expected from you? And the true priviledges and rights you have in Him?

Christ's Blessings.

Israel Chukwuka Okunwaye

PART I:

THE GOD OF THE GOSPEL

This book– divided into three parts, is about faith in Jesus Christ of Nazareth, the messiah; concerning what it means to receive the divine life of God now, and to walk in His blazing light of righteousness and love. Also, a contemplation of eternal life hereafter, and genuine prospect of Christ's return. This is a classic for the one in sincere quest of faith– and for the believer of Jesus Christ [the Son of the living God]; as a worthy reference tool and a reminder of the necessity of the gospel of Christ. A work for my generation and beyond. It is more than a story about Jesus, it's the essence of His life and unnegotiable relevance it holds for your soul. The work relies heavily on the Bible, but in some parts it has a reference that refers to some academic materials to further buttress a scriptural point, and for the purpose of examining a critical thought, as needful not as though mandatory, but which some may find helpful in their perusing. We can do nothing against the precious word of God but for it. I hope you mix the word of faith from the written word with faith, so it profits you.

Let's begin.

I

HAVE FAITH IN GOD THROUGH CHRIST

Declaring the excellency and Lordship of Jesus Christ of Nazareth, the Son of the Living God

Jeremiah 33:3 says, 'Call to Me, and I will answer you, and show you great and mighty things, which you do not know.'

Romans 10:13 says, 'for, "Everyone who calls on the name of the Lord will be saved". '

Why put our hope in God other than ourselves? Why trust what Christ says of Himself? Bold, audacious, distinct and outrageous claim of being God's Son, and of Him being the true and only revelation of Jehovah God? His emphasis and directness are glaring and unapologetic. He compels us to realise our inadequacies but His sufficiency, as we examine the evidences before us. Everything written before was foretelling Him and paving our eternal salvation. Some important considerations:

I. To come to conclusions, I suggest we consider the overwhelming weight of historical and documentary evidence that point to the real existence of Jesus Christ in the flesh, as well as credible philosophical underpinnings making a case for God,[1] prophecies preceding Him, and of the presence of supernatural acts of God defying human explanation when He appeared. From as God in baby form and born of a virgin, to His demonstrated power guiding a community of people who believed His works. These all leaves great room for contemplation. Even beyond these time framed axes.

II. Also, consider the evidence of the presence of evil and sin in our world. As light point to the presence of darkness, which it eliminates, similarly, where good exist there is the opposing force of evil. But God in His power excels over Satan's devices. The conflict of pain and joy tells us that there is a pattern of control that no one escapes from– of birth and death. We are all born to die– as a seed dying in earth's nature is to live and blossom under the right conditions, so God's design is for humans to be translated to His nature of endless and divine life in His righteousness. I highlight these contrasts, so we see not so much the order in nature or in our lives, but the one that ordered it. There is a saying, you make your bed how you want to lie on it. It is a sense of the ability in man to organise, innovate or create things in some scale. Most people would think it untenable to suggest that food cooked itself, or engines sort themselves out without external inputs. How much more nature's intricate system, of the earth and the heavens, of its precision and constancy, of heat and cold, of wet and dry periods. Who set it in motion? God says He did. This is not a matter of tinkering with what exists, or manufacturing from it. It's setting the stars in its place and drawing the lines in each leaf or fin. Well, God says He did. You didn't. I didn't. To accept that is to solve a significant chunk of unnecessary unbelief right there, that being a no-brainer.

We must accept also the limitedness and constant reviews of our knowledge, the measured nature of our strength and power, when placed in comparison with the glories of Christ. I recall years ago speaking about the beauty of creation, and someone took the view that whatever existed as in the case of a garden, did because someone always designed it, whilst taking God completely out of the picture. As though to prove He had some stake He had to literally 'photobomb' the picture in debate. Rather than fester to the extremes I have always wondered why it is so challenging to see the providence of God on one hand, and the skill to tend on the other. A necessary balance. Even though God could upset it if He prefers. Come to think of it, who shaped the beauty of the mountains? Made the flowers? The seeds? And so on. Before someone hurries to manufacture a genetically enhanced seed to counter this point, just pause and think original. The first and authentic, from which other inspiration arise— and yes, many things, some seemingly improved, but also taking cognisance some contrary, defective, diseased semblances have sprung too, which had had to be put down in some cases; other experiments remain in the lab. Point being made is God made these things we see on the earth, crops, animals, landscapes, ocean etc and what He made, He made it good. He has even given man the intellectual ability to do great things on the platform of His goodness. We have a responsibility as those placed here to tend, till, nourish our God-given garden [earth] for His glory. Rather than often factor God out, what about giving Him the credit, and doing our part to protect our environment, and acknowledge the Creator. Though man has neglected his duty and brought the earth all manner of misery through unhelpful activities, God promises to restore. Because of sin and its evil, and corruption, decay has set it in on the earth and also affected her inhabitants– but surely there is a God-plan to fix all things. It is always nice and wise to give thanks and recognise the one from whom all blessings flow!

In one of my outdoor evangelical outreaches in the streets of Birmingham, in Five ways this time, I met a young man willing to engage on the subject concerning faith as I stood at the subway park, waiting and watching cars and buses plying the roads, whilst occasionally whispering a prayer and looking for an interested person. I must say, it's a little bit rare I find one as this young man before me. We spoke for a decent few minutes. He wanted to talk, not just walk away with the leaflet. He introduced himself as having scientific leanings, and as one conversant with some biblical dogmas and individual based beliefs. Basically, he said, I have a belief system, you have yours, and others have theirs, so why should I change mine for yours and others theirs for mine! In his view, it does not make sense. As I listened to him and we conversed, it occurred to me in my frequent evangelistic interactions, both outdoors and in my online spaces, these questions and reservations have often sprung up. Also, only recently at a training I attended in Brierley Hill, Dudley in the West Midlands of England, put together by a community service outfit to support efforts at awareness of human and social rights, and provide community support. During the break for social interaction, a group of four got together, I was seating just opposite, and they strayed into the subject of religion. I had a pin on my jacket, a pin of the Cross, a reminder of the work of Christ. I didn't feel any of them felt threatened by my faith or forcefully indoctrinated. It however got them talking about the role of religion in society, it wasn't long before they wanted my input too, which was gracious, though I can't say I subconsciously suggested the trajectory of the thinking. Possibly. You will find out that few times do people in an office space engage over religion in 21st century Europe. It is rare, from my limited observation, at least in few interactive moments at gatherings at seminars, trainings, work, celebratory engagements, get togethers etc (apart from Christian ministry engagements). I have noted in these secular spaces conversation on sports, politics, gardening, relationships, weather reports, someone else's attitude, or just on work a bit passively– come up as top chat item. But on God, that's the tough one. I concede however if discussions in any circumstance growingly becomes politely toxic, I would prefer to extricate myself– as such usually ends nowhere.

I perceive revival is the awakening of the mind to God-matters, to ask questions, the yearning to know, and then seeing a heavenly influence. God can reach your community where you live but can also affect nations in a now globalised world, but even importantly, He can reach you as an individual and bless your soul, as though it's just your interest He desires. I think God many a time begins to work when we invite in our lives and community, but often the decider is what do one do with a God-moment or time of visitation. God shows up in often strange ways, He attracted Prophet Moses's attention in the wilderness by a strange occurrence, and the Ethiopian by Evangelist Philip's question— 'can you figure out what you are reading?' Christian conversations are opportunities to meet God, especially when there is someone in there willing to engage and with right answers. Anyway, we were here to engage on matters of social relevance, this had to be one. After they had carried on for about 15-20 minutes I thought I could say something now, because I wasn't sure earlier where the conversation was going and if my contribution would not be despised.

Nonetheless, I felt a gentle prompting in my heart to say something, even more because only the previous night as I prayed with my family, we had asked God to give us opportunities in the week for the gospel and to show God's love. Now this was it. I said, can I just add— 'I believe there is no air, that's just my belief!' I said it with all the energy I could muster and with a straight face, and then sat down. They looked at me, and were 'like really?' with 'how could you say that' expression. They paused a bit, seeing I wasn't flinching, and then laughed as they finally got my sarcasm. Obviously, it will not be right to say that. Of course, I added it wasn't material I had a strong confident conviction about my concocted fact but that it didn't change the real fact. In essence, I could not just insist I have a set of beliefs but also responsibility was on me to inquire as to the truth of that belief. I again added, that for some that was a journey of a life time seeking to discover truth, but need not be, as the truth was in the bible already, God's word to us, as Christ has revealed God to us. After this the room had a natural calm and smiles around. I knew God had started out something– it was time for more tea and coffee. Which is always a nice relief. It was this memorable story I was able to bring back to explain to the friend I met on the street, on the need to examine the range of beliefs he had and not hold on to them tenaciously, unproven. He got it. He said to me, I just kick-started him on a journey of faith, and he would explore further. It was time for him to go, I shook him and wished him God's speed. On that same place, I have had the priviledge to pray for some who heard me and wanted to give their hearts to Christ, immediately. Some had to take home something to ponder about. I have also honestly met some who could not be fussed. This story is not farfetched from responding to questions from a visitor to a Church service desiring to know God better. On whatever platform, in the pulpit, coffee shop, secular work space, or street- it is important to know God loves us and do not impose His love, but we have a choice to choose to explore His truth and grow spiritually, but I warn you, it would knock down any baseless foundation you may've had. They say different strokes for different folks– but when it comes to biblical scripture, I have always believed it could enrich the soul of any one who gives the chance for the Holy Spirit to work on their heart. Again, this must be made of a free willing choice. Beloved, we have to repent in our mind by reneging on principles or beliefs that have guided our lives, where the merits do not hold water, where it is contrary to the word of God. Just the same way you would not hold on to a culture that is not beneficial or unsafe. This is God's path, to follow what is needful and true.

On historic evidence and human limitations

'The integrity of any ancient writing is determined by the number of documented manuscripts or fragments of manuscript which still exists.'[2] There is a consensus on the above assessment. I think it appeals to good reason. Bible scholars have pointed out the Bible was written in a period span of about

1600 years by numerous God-believing authors, who mostly had first hand encounters with these recorded supernatural events. This resulted in the 66 books, endorsed by early Church fathers. The chosen books are considered the most relevant, complimentary of each of the others, and by those whose account are true to the lived experiences (like being there with Christ). Also, phenomenal is, they were men whose incredible ministries and involvement in the national life of the ancient Jewish nation, as the covenant people of God according to the promise to Abraham, were detailed. These texts have been attested to by well over 5000 New Testament (NT) Greek manuscripts since, and over 10,000 Latin NT manuscripts.[3] These copies ensure the accounts are not edited or misrepresented, for example, the Codex Vaticanus and Codex Siniaticus, which are parchment copies of the NT of the 4th Century (AD 325-450).[4] Similarly the dead sea scrolls of the Old Testament (OT) contained inscribed fragments and were found in Qumran in AD 68. Also, external sources affirm the existence of these writings and stories. The Jewish Talmud (has texts of the OT) which is said to have been reproduced in AD 270-500.[5] Also ancient historians and philosophers as Tacitus in AD 110 wrote on the persecution of Christians on account of Jesus,[6] as also, its' been noted one Flavius Josephus in his time documented about

Christ's fame. It is sufficient to say that it is undisputable an actual person called Jesus Christ lived, rather than it been a made-up story. Perhaps, this is a good start point for some.

Dear reader, consider even in traditions, were predominantly oral history is recognised, how much more were there is a body of documented evidences from the past. I am sure some cultures find this endearing too. Both are weighty. Sound logic suggests we do not discountenance such evidences. It is not difficult to accept an oral tradition of the ancient times if such stories were so notorious [notable, of common knowledge] and leaves an undeniable impression of significant proportion. It is told to one generation who then passes it on to the next and onwards. Even more notable, were noble men of repute handle such with great care and transparency. To reduce it to writing or markings will be to preserve the idea even further. It is worth noting that neither oral stories, writings or perhaps vast archaeological discoveries can always give 100% satisfaction of accuracy, to prove deception has not been advanced from the onset, and mass produced. Was it tampered with? Often the evidence for, exceeds the argument against. If one feels otherwise, then the burden is on such a person to provide contrary magnanimous evidence to clearly show the contrary, or honestly be quiet. These existing evidences provides a very good place to start. And where true, as in the case of scriptural texts, it becomes a great resource. The next step becomes debating and examining the content of the evidence. However, it will be impossible to denounce an account which has many witnesses.[7]

II

THE STRENGTH OF GOD'S GRACE

In contemporary times the word 'grace' is tagged alone messiness and weakness, and rarely a revelation of strength. Grace scripturally is the power of Christ's redemption. It is the strength of God at work in us who believe. This perspective encourages us to see grace not as for some feeble folks as though any is strong without it. Grace makes you strong and equipped.

2 Corinthians 12:9 says, 'And he said unto me, My grace (*a reference to that which is gratifying, acceptable, joyous and gracious– it is 'the divine influence upon the heart, and its reflection in the life'*) is sufficient (enough, satisfactory) for thee: for my strength (*dunamis*– miraculous power, mighty, violence) is made perfect (to finish, fulfil, complete) in weakness (feebleness of body and mind, disease, illness, infirmities, weak). Most gladly therefore will I

rather glory (rejoice, boast) in my infirmities, that the power of Christ may rest upon me.' (I have inserted the meanings to certain keywords).

In the scripture, Apostle Paul shares with us that the fullness of God's power is revealed in us despite our weakness, in our fragility– 2 Corinthians 4:7. This is so God could take the utmost glory. It is God using us though there is work yet still to be done in us, not being perfect in the flesh, but having a perfect Spirit at work in the believer of Jesus Christ. This is the triumph of faith. As our faith is reposed in a faithful Christ, His righteousness and power become what upholds and redeems us. God intends we become as He is and reveal the greatness of His power.

What happens when the almighty God's power shines in us, it dispels darkness, so Christ is seen at work through us! The Lord Jesus said, in Matthew 5:16 *'Let your light so shine before men, that they may see your good works and glorify your father in heaven.'* We don't cease being human, but the power of sin is broken. No believer plans or enjoys sin, rather they seek to please God; also, if they err they are enlightened and humble to seek an ever-merciful God, whose grace is assured to heal and strengthen.

Apostle Paul tells us of 'a man' who comes to understanding of aspects of the wisdom of God, for we all know in part, according to the measure granted us by God. He speaks this of himself but is cautious to not boast in this wisdom as his, but, glorifies God. He even goes further to speak of his weakness, sharing with us a 'thorn in his flesh,' a weakness, a restraint which we do not know in specifics. What we know that whatever that he struggled with in the flesh and prayed about three times for God to take away, but God wouldn't, as that it was opportunity for Christ to show His power. And, also, for him not to be exalted above measure! Is this a Jacob's leap from a broken hip? Is it Apostle Peter's memory of his betrayal of the Lord but at same time knowing His forgiveness forever and testifying of His power? Is it the blind man from birth in John 9:1-12 who is so for the glory of God at an appointed time?

This I know, that the power of God in any situation brings total victory. But God, is able to work, and walk in ways that His sovereign will permits for the best good He knows. I am reminded of Prophet Moses, God shows him the divine fire, that burns in a bush but do not consume it. God who is a consuming fire burns up every rubble but, in this instance, decides it burns with the bush. It is glory that it consumes the bush, but greater glory that it burns in the midst of it, and the bush stays alive. How can a great God live in mortal flesh and not destroy it– one word, grace! Like Apostle Paul in Judges 6:11-16 Gideon receives the promise of God to see His power even though he was weak. In any case who is strong without God? Would you let God work in you today for His glory?

III

THERE IS DIVINE POWER IN CHRIST'S GRACE. IT WILL STRENGTHEN YOUR HEART TO SERVE GOD

This 'God's goodness–' we can rely on it. Always. The scripture says, *'Jesus Christ is the same yesterday and today and forever. Do not be carried away by all kinds of strange teachings. It is good for our hearts to be strengthened by grace, not by eating ceremonial foods, which is of no benefit to those who do so.'* Hebrews 13:8-9

It is on the revelation of Christ we stand as believers, that the one who gave Himself, He is the anchor for your soul. He is true and the same forevermore. It is through Christ we receive the favour and mercy of God, become completely acquitted from our sins and declared righteous before an ever-faithful God. It is typical of a weight of expectation and burden being lifted from off one's shoulders. Christ offers and gives strength to broken hearts. As it is written, 'It is good for our hearts to be strengthened by grace!' It is delightful, it is wholesome. Do not lose sight of Christ to depend on ceremonial laws as though your justification come therewith. Your fulfilment, sufficiency, approval, sanctification, strengthening is from Christ alone. In the early Church, some were about to be derailed by foisting a thinking that their salvation was contingent on other valid performances, what they eat, their clothing choice, observance of traditional stipulations according to biblical Jewish norms in that instance (as in the old testament), whether they were of the circumcision or not. These additions were not necessarily on this instance wrong or sinful, but when they begin to distract from the glory that is in the Lord Jesus Christ, putting the brethren in bondage again, it becomes imperative for a godly reminder to hold fast to the faith which is in Christ, for therein lies our victory.

To the Galatians Apostle Paul wrote incisively:

'See with what large letters I have written to you with my own hand! As many as desire to make a good showing in the flesh, these would compel you to be circumcised, only that they may not suffer persecution for the cross of Christ. For not even those who are circumcised keep the

law, but they desire to have you circumcised that they may boast in your flesh. But God forbid that I should boast except in the cross of our Lord Jesus Christ, by whom the world has been crucified to me, and I to the world. For in Christ Jesus neither circumcision nor uncircumcision avails anything, but a new creation. And as many as walk according to this rule, peace and mercy be upon them, and upon the Israel of God.' Galatians 6:11-16.

The key here is not to exalt anything, person or practice over the supremacy of Christ. The systems and dogmas of the world is now dead, crucified, to us who believe. We have no connection with it, and its influence gone with it. Therefore it 'avails nothing' before God. By adhering to it as a law for justification we get no just rewards for such labours. Else we will be boasting in our achievements by our hand rather than in the power of His grace. The light of God needs to shine on such motive for purification. His divine intervention is what makes the difference. Also, I am reminded of the words of Christ Himself, to not have a tenacious hold to traditions, whatever that may be, that conflicts with His words, or allow for it to gain upper ground.

In Luke 24:39-46,

'Jesus went out as usual to the Mount of Olives, and his disciples followed him. On reaching the place, he said to them, 'Pray that you will not fall into temptation. He withdrew about a stone's throw beyond them, knelt down and prayed, 'Father, if you are willing, take this cup from me; yet not my will, but yours be done.' An angel from heaven appeared to him and strengthened him. And being in anguish, he prayed more earnestly, and his sweat was like drops of blood falling to the ground.

When he rose from prayer and went back to the disciples, he found them asleep, exhausted from sorrow. 'Why are you sleeping? he asked them. 'Get up and pray so that you will not fall into temptation.'

Apostle Paul prayed for strength on our 'inner man,' that place that drives our outward experiences. Within our soul. My prayer is, dear Lord let your glorious light shine continually. The man or woman in union with Christ in the Spirit by faith in God's word, is born again, a new creation, because of the life of God that has come to dwell in them. Not that they change physically but a change has occurred already in them. Ephesians 3:14-21 tells us, *'For this cause I bow my knees unto the Father of our Lord Jesus Christ, of whom the whole family in heaven and earth is named, that he would grant you, according to the riches of his glory, to be strengthened with might by his Spirit in the inner man; that Christ may dwell in your hearts by faith; that ye, being rooted and grounded in love, may be able to comprehend with all saints what is the breadth, and length, and depth, and height; and to know the love of Christ, which passeth knowledge, that ye might be filled with all the fulness of God. Now unto him that is able to do exceeding abundantly above all that we ask or think, according to the power that worketh in us, unto him be glory in the church by Christ Jesus throughout all ages, world without end. Amen.'*

Indeed, God has said that, it is not by power nor might, but His Spirit. This is true today.

Emphasis on key thoughts concerning the strength of God's grace:

We have seen how God assures Apostle Paul of His strength in the midst of persecution and life's challenges– of His perfect strength in weakness. We have also seen how God assures the Ephesian Church and a prophetic word that He is able to strengthen the inner man, our body being the temple of the Lord by His Holy Spirit and fire, a promise for those who believe. We also see that even our Lord is enabled by the strength of the Holy Spirit for the ultimate sacrifice of redeeming man through the death and resurrection on the Cross.

It seems to me the scripture is clearly replete of men and women who accomplished great things by the Spirit of God and the strength He supplies.

Whether we consider a Gideon who was the least in his tribe but raised of God to help the nation Israel in time of crisis, or a Moses who stammered and crossed between cultures and orientations— of Midian and united in marriage to Zipporah, Jethro's daughter, him being nursed in the Egyptian King's court to his prime, and yet of Hebrew heritage. His split allegiances did not stop God using him to bring deliverance to a people suppressed in bondage. Do we then speak of King David often outnumbered in battle and opened to many betrayals and yet saw God rescuing power. One has to pause as one reads through the scriptures to reflect on the goodness and strength of God.

It is His grace that saves us. Romans 5:6-8, '*Now hope does not disappoint, because the love of God has been poured out in our hearts by the Holy Spirit who was given to us. For when we were still without strength, in due time Christ died for the ungodly. For scarcely for a righteous man will one die; yet perhaps for a good man someone would even dare to die. But God demonstrates His own love toward us, in that while we were still sinners, Christ died for us.*' Herein is the grace of God, as it becomes our help and strength to serve the living God. We had no strength or ability in ourselves. Ephesians 2:8-9, 'For by grace you have been saved through faith, and that not of yourselves; it is the gift of God, not of works, lest anyone should boast.' In Jude 20-25 we see again the need to hold steadfast to the confession of our faith as believers but reminds us that it is strength of God that keeps us in Him. We acknowledge our responsibility to believe the gospel and walk in the truth of it, but in humility we also recognise that it has been God working all the while, before, during and after our conversion. That it is by Him alone we nurse this precious hope of eternity with our Lord Jesus Christ.

IV

GOD CREATES OPPORTUNITY FOR THE GOSPEL TO THRIVE– THIS IS MEANT FOR YOU

'And He (Jesus Christ) said to them, 'what kind of conversation is this that you have with one another as you walk and are sad?' Then the one whose name was Cleopas answered and said to Him, 'Are you the only stranger in Jerusalem, and have you not known the things which happened these days?' And He said to them, 'what things?' So they said to Him, 'The things concerning Jesus of Nazareth, who was a Prophet mighty in deed and word before God and all the people...' Luke 24:17-19.

Miracles are not just healings, but events that defy natural occurrences– supernatural moments beyond known natural ability, inspired by the Holy Spirit. When the dead comes back to life after three days, or the feeble have victory over the strong or a 'legion of Roman soldiers,' then before you is the need for explanation and awe. The bible has many of such incredible stories. Ephesians 3:20 reminds us first and foremost of a powerful God who is able! The extent of which cannot be weighed in human terms– at best to a narrow capacity. Blows your mind? A God should. Else, create your 'gods–' or puppets. The living God works, beyond imaginations, beyond requests, thought streams, desires, only because He is all-mighty God. I sense as God permeates the subconscious and subliminal realms, the consciously-driven motives, and unspoken gestures, that we discover His purpose is to enrich our hearts with his love and vitality for an un-contradictory dependence on him. So that the confession of our faith may be more evident. This way, the world will know our confession is not a mockery of ideas and ideals, of human-sourced strength or construct, or a game show, and then Christ take all the glory for His work.

In this season, two things have been impressed on my heart, that God is able to answer prayers to shine His glory across the nations and take the glory. Also, that he could endorse organisational structures, programmes and campaigns, but He could also skip all that, including treaties, routines and tactical spins to reach hearts directly, if He chooses. He sends His word but also creates the space for it to thrive. He calls His servants but also speaks the word, and makes the spoken word bear fruit. In the written word, we see one plants to create a platform for the hearing of the word, another 'waters,' equips, encourage as a result of the transforming word of Christ, but overall God makes the word have impact. He also enables the planter to plant seeds of hope, the encourager and teacher to do it with grace and wisdom– not shallow words with a guise of intellect but authentically bereft of godly impetus or genuine intelligence for the higher minds, but a word which is by virtue of divine imputation (for God's wisdom is greater than the world's). God is the one working altogether in this, so that the appetite for Jesus Christ with be wetted, so many will see the great spirit of Christ for themselves only through the inspiration of the bible, and that by the cords of His Spirit pull the hearer to Himself.

When opportunity comes such as this, the human mind immediately fathoms how can I harness this [for material gain]– but why? Moments like this are to be cherished and reflected on, if you see the purpose of God. It is like 'Manna–' what do we do with this? Of what significance? Luke 24 story of

Jesus's conversation with some guys about the gossip in town about how He has made an incredible sacrifice and the promise to defy death. The miracle was not so much the talk but the God in it, but also because of what He did in the preaching of the word and divine evidence, also the thrill of what God could do (or rather has done as He had had the sacrifice perfected, while all that rambling was on)– something had definitely engulfed the land. But why all this, God wanted everyone's attention for soul redemption. So it wasn't time to make merchandise of the gospel or good news but for the cross to eternally change lives. In Acts chapters 9, 10, 11 we see God setting up occasions to make many hear the gospel. God makes sure Ananias meets Paul by speaking to him by revelation, so he ministers to him and prays for him. Ananias at first didn't want to meet with Paul, as he was a persecutor of believers of Jesus, but he changes his mind. Same for Cornelius-Peter scenario. Sometimes some think its coincidence to meet someone who they happen to have the chance to talk about faith in Jesus Christ– I believe God is working behind the scenes to ensure questions are answered. He sets people up to have opportunities to hear the true gospel, dispel false doctrines they have adhered to beforehand and develop their faith. Wisdom is to make the most of this opportunity, redeem the time as its 'day' not 'night,' and let salvation come into your heart today. Supernatural occurrences are just to get your attention so that God can speak into you– if it gets you to search more about Him, praise God. This journey is good, and could be life changing, if you believe that Jesus Christ is who He says He is. The saviour of human souls and redeemer of mankind– He is Lord and the son of the living God. Now, that changes everything forever. In His time, all things are beautiful, trust Him.

V

KNOWING YOUR GOD

'... But the people who know their God will show their strength and stand against him.' Daniel 11:32 NLV

Do you know God can multiply your 'five loaves of bread and two fishes' and bring about more? Don't think the size of your gift, think Great God! So any time you deal with the God, remember to entrust to Him your 'giftings,' He can do more with it! No matter how much it is. Praise God for it and for His power to do awesome things. One of the ways to gain victory is by understanding the plan of the enemy, not being naïve, but rather putting it to shame through trusting Jesus Christ. What is the enemy's plan? It is to choke your mind through lies of worthlessness, or perhaps flattery meant to discomfit you in the end, to steal your joy, distract your progress and where possible destroy you. But you have to know God is for you. He is on your side.

The word of God exposes it in John 10:10, 'The robber comes only to steal and kill and to destroy. I came so they might have life, a great full life.' You know, the work of Jesus, is for you. Shake your mind, receive it, it is meant for you no matter who you think you are. Satan, an evil spirit may attempt to rob you of this satisfaction for your soul which is part of your body, but reject that pattern of thought and confess Christ's truth.

A lesson: when the spirit of deception and wickedness is at work, you don't renegotiate your place in God instead you tackle it headlong by knowing and declaring what God says about you, and what He has promised by His eternal name to do through you. God has given the believer of Jesus Christ who is yielded to Him, soundness of mind, the grace to discern the purpose of God upon the earth. The enemy is not just any person, the big picture is the spirit that have taken residence or influence their actions. The spiritual strategy is to bind that force or manipulation in the name of Jesus Christ and reject it. Operate from the stand point of victory. Why? Because Jesus Christ won on the cross, so in His authority you declare the will of the Almighty God upon the earth, by faith in Him.

Ephesians 6:12– *'Our fight is not with people. It is against the leaders and the powers and the spirits of darkness in this world. It is against the demon world that works in the heavens.'*

Once you identify the lies of the enemy towards you and his tactics, engage in a spiritual assault by prayer, and confession of truth over your mind. This will help you grow in the grace of Jesus Christ. Halleluyah! Praise Jesus Christ who has all powers in heaven and earth. In His name we have conquered and are more than conquerors. Amen

VI

WHO IS YOUR GOD?

I once had another chance to talk to someone about my faith– what came across was that my God was merciful, gracious, able to save sinners and powerful to determine the eternal destiny of human souls. No sooner, others around watching, joined in the conversation and claimed that though their faith was not of the Christian orientation, they did not see why what I worshipped differed in strong terms from what they believed. Basically, we all seem to have confidence in a spiritual being greater than ourselves, with endearing attributes. What broke the ice was when I asked if their 'God' was the father of our Lord Jesus Christ. 'Oh no,' they said–

'Our God has got no son or a wife.' What became clear was, either that the God we served had a fundamental difference, or they were oblivious to what they worshipped. With the God I serve nothing is impossible, so He can operate outside the laws of nature, which He gave. It would be contradictory then to set up a logic and question His ability to defy it. He has chosen to operate under certain immutable divine love, and cannot stand against Himself– this includes His sovereign will. The line is drawn, as the bible teaches that God became flesh in the person of Jesus Christ, and that anyone who believes in Him comes into a life-saving relationship, forgiven from sin. Understanding the divinity of Christ unlocks our knowledge of God– in fact it is everything of real worth. It shows us who He is, His identity. As He is not just a human being or Carpenter's son, Prophet or teacher (*Rabbi*), a miracle worker of some sort and someone just significant in history– rather He is God-revealed. He is connected to the divine. He is alive today, and involved in our daily lives. Jesus once had a conversation centred on what people thought of him in Matthew 16:13-17 (NLV)– 'Jesus came into the country of Caesarea Philippi. He asked His followers, 'Who do people say that I, the Son of Man, am?' They said, 'Some say You are John the Baptist and some say Elijah and others say Jeremiah or one of the early preachers.' He said to them, 'But who do you say that I am?' Simon Peter said, 'You are the Christ, the Son of the living God.' Jesus said to him, 'Simon, son of Jonah, you are happy because you did not learn this from man. My Father in heaven has shown you this.'

Who is this Jesus Christ? He is Lord, and the son of the living God as Peter declared and affirmed by Christ Himself. To disagree with this view, is to contend with what Christ said of Himself. And He is not a liar. We are familiar with the saying that God made heaven and earth. But consider this scripture– 'Christ is the visible image of the invisible God. He existed before anything was created and is supreme over all creation, for through him God created everything in the heavenly realms and on earth. He made the things we can see and the things we can't see— such as thrones, kingdoms, rulers, and authorities in the unseen world. Everything was created through Him and for Him.
He existed before anything else, and he holds all creation together. Christ is also the head of the church, which is His body. He is the beginning, supreme over all who rise from the dead. So He is first in everything.' Colossians 1:15-18 (NLT)

You see then Christ is of God, bound up in divine union. You cannot accept the almighty God and deny Jesus Christ. To serve the true God is to serve the God who is the father of our Lord Jesus Christ of Nazareth– who is of the lineage of King David, the messiah and the redeemer of mankind who rely on His righteousness. So, I ask again, is your God the father of our lord and saviour Jesus Christ? Anyone who disagrees on this, agrees there is a difference in the God we serve, and also missing a core knowledge of Him. Being anti-Christ is being anti-God. No one worships God and denies Him– this is why this matter has to be resolved in your heart if not done already. God requires in this time, in this age, we worship Him according to knowledge, the knowledge of His Son. God's gift to you is Jesus Christ, Himself revealed.

VII

HOW GOD LEADS BY HIS GOODNESS AND PURPOSE

James 1:3, 13, 17; Luke 4:12-13; Jeremiah 17:10; 1 John 4:1.

When we come before our Lord, we come to receive instruction for life. To understand our place in Him is based entirely on His goodness, and His great love for us. His love saves us, and keeps us in His divine purpose. In understanding His nature, albeit in a measure by His grace, as revealed in His word, we are able to appreciate His glory and anticipate His direction. By understanding His will we know God do not set evil traps for us to prove our commitment to Him, He rather pours us with daily mercies, goodness and faithfulness, urging us on in triumph. He sets us in a prepared place of His grace, in a secure and fenced territory of his protection. It is being under His sovereign and outstretched wings. Satan on the flipside tempts us with evil, to lure us away from the plan of God. He is the one who challenges our credibility and seeks to prove your unfitness by presenting foul options, and then goes on to accuse you. God instead derides giving us opportunities for failure. He won't give us more than we can handle. If we find ourselves practicing any evil deeds, it isn't because He has not made a way of escape, but rather our weakness has caught up with us, again He would come to the rescue. He tempts no one with evil, He refuses to be tempted as well with evil. He proves our genuineness and competence, by His goodness. He gives us opportunities to serve, and rewards us with more when we excel in our commitment to each task. First, if faithful in small, then He commits more. This is not the skewed sense of wide interpretation [or obscure pattern] of 'it is not what you do but who you are,' creating room for tribal prejudices, rather it is a real sense of interpretation of who a believer is *in God* and also a just reward for faithfulness for all. If He asks us to sacrifice our lives or what we hold dear, it is because He gave us anyway, and often He intends to see our heart yielded to Him more than the gift we offer.

As a believer, to set a trap or evil test, to prove another is not consistent with God's character. What we should do is to commit to others credible opportunities, and offers in goodness, where they excel in the little, and then reward justly with more. But to create hate, strife, resentment, or any evil to prove another, is sheer manipulation and not the Spirit of Christ. It's spiritually unintelligent. What God calls us to do is discern and test spirits by the word, to see if there is sincerity and whether such a person is operating in honour of God. The word of God is divine and key, as we evaluate a conduct by reference to what the word says. God leads the way in this as we see in Adam, Saul, David, Job, Abraham and many more, He shows them His goodness and then rewards their faithfulness, where they represent Him faithfully He commits more to them and keeps His promise. He is committed to meeting your need not just what you want or prefer. But be sure His utmost desire is to grant you deep and true satisfaction. In Christ, we know the love of God, that He is not trying to get you, He is not seeing if you are not good enough by asking you to do something foolish or wrong. In fact, it is His goodness that pulls us. So when you hear any evil prompting in your heart, rebuke it and ask God to show you the right way. Every good and perfect gift comes from only God, devoid of deception, and full of mercy. When any evil befalls you, God has not sent it, the enemy of your faith is at work at that instance, discern it and counter it in prayer and by formidable trust in God's faithfulness. We live in an evil and fallen world– we may ask, as God is all powerful, why does He allow certain ills? We maybe should also ask, why does He intervene sometimes to stop evil sweeps or bring victory when we pray? One thing we know for certain and most reassuringly is that a day is coming, which He has promised to bring victory by judgement, over all evil and Satan, establishing His kingdom, then we will see Him face to face and every knee will bow to His authority. Also true, and not inconsistent, is the victory we have now in the spirit by faith in Christ, and because we believe the kingdom of God reigns on the earth through us. His will and purpose is done through us by His Holy Spirit, we are indeed His representatives, sons, His people on earth doing His bidding. Now we know in part, and we experience a measure of this divine presence knowing that even in this life God walks with us, by His spirit, therefore we can expect not just His intervention. For our body is His temple and abode. We have become His precious hands and feet to bring healing to the nations. He promises in His name we have His divine authority. So let's know our Lord wishes us well, and is not playing games with our commitment to Him, and let us treat one another that way. Even when persecution arises, it is the attack of the enemy, to stiffen the flow of the word and destroy our faith. In response– we should pray that we might be continually bold, carry on the work till Jesus comes, encourage one another, possibly– flee to another place if persecution arises till it abates, or instead pray for significant deliverances from the wicked one, not fighting in the flesh but trusting the spirit at work. If after all, it seems the Lord allows it to persist, to know in His sovereign will, He intends to grow us and bring ultimately great glory to His name, and that yet still His peace beyond understanding and comfort remains by His spirit, and our reward awaits. By His grace, the response is always one of joy haven been counted worthy for the ministry, and to share in His plan. If our heart grows weak, know His power upholds and strengthens. Lastly, I will say to any, whose faith in God is in doubt, wavering, because you are discouraged because you think God should have acted, or the pressures of life has placed a demand you cannot fulfil, I invite you to see that God has been the unseen hand fighting for you all the while. Give Him the glory due, and enjoy His love.

VIII

GOD IS DIFFERENT FROM MAN– HE SPEAKS AND THINKS HIGHLY OF YOU: 'THE GOD WHO ACKNOWLEDGES'

'But there is a place where someone has testified: 'What is mankind that you are mindful of them, a son of man that you care for him?' Hebrew 2: 6 (Psalm 8:1-9)

'I thank my God, making mention of you always in my prayers, hearing of your love and faith which you have toward the Lord Jesus and toward all the saints, that the sharing of your faith may become effective by the acknowledgment of every good thing which is in you in Christ Jesus.' Philemon 1:5-6

'Paul and Barnabas stayed there a long time preaching with the strength the Lord gave. <u>God helped them to do</u>

powerful works when they preached which showed He was with them.' Acts 14:3

I call Him the God who acknowledges what you are in Him, and what you could become if you fully depend on Him, by bearing witness He sent and anointed you and called you into relationship with Him. We ought to share in this disposition. No one operating by human strength can function in this realm. It is surely evident from scriptures that God treasures the human race. He has put man in dominion over all created things. I delight myself in understanding that God delights and speaks highly of me. And true, for you as well if you believe in Him. Some instances, would give us a minute glimpse of this incredible predisposition.

Of Jesus Christ, God says— *'This is <u>My beloved Son, in whom I am well-pleased</u>.' Matthew 3:16-17*

Concerning Job, in a conversation—

'The LORD said to Satan, 'Have you considered <u>My servant Job? For there is no one like him on the earth</u>, a blameless and upright man, fearing God and turning away from evil.' Then Satan answered the LORD, 'Does Job fear God for nothing? 'Have You not made a hedge about him and his house and all that he has, on every side?...' Job 1:8-11

Concerning King David there is a wonderful testimony, in Acts 13:21-23 –

'*Then they asked for a king, and God gave them Saul the son of Kish, a man of the tribe of Benjamin, for forty years.' After He had removed him, He raised up David to be their king, concerning <u>whom He also testified and said, 'I have found David the son of Jesse, a man after my heart, who will do all my will.'</u> 'From the descendants of this man, according to promise, God has brought to Israel a Saviour, Jesus'*

Of Abraham– '*The* LORD *said,* '<u>*Shall I hide from Abraham what I am about to do,*</u> *since Abraham will surely become a great and mighty nation, and in him all the nations of the earth will be blessed?' Genesis 18:17-18*

To the nation Israel, we understand from *Psalm 105:7-15–*

'*He is the* LORD *our God;*
His judgments are in all the earth.
<u>*He remembers His covenant forever,*</u>
The word which He commanded, for a thousand generations,
The covenant which He made with Abraham,
And His oath to Isaac,
And confirmed it to Jacob for a statute,
<u>*To Israel as an everlasting covenant,*</u>
<u>*Saying, 'To you I will give the land of Canaan*</u>
<u>*As the allotment of your inheritance,'*</u>
When they were few in number,
Indeed very few, and strangers in it.

When they went from one nation to another,
From one kingdom to another people,
He permitted no one to do them wrong;
Yes, He rebuked kings for their sakes,
Saying, 'Do not touch My anointed ones,
And do My prophets no harm."

To the gentiles redeemed by faith–

Acts 10:34- 43

'So Peter opened his mouth and said: 'Truly I
understand that God shows no partiality, but in every
nation anyone who fears him and does what is right is
acceptable to him. As for the word that he sent to Israel,
preaching good news of peace through Jesus Christ (he is
Lord of all), you yourselves know what happened
throughout all Judea, beginning from Galilee after the
baptism that John proclaimed: how God anointed Jesus
of Nazareth with the Holy Spirit and with power. He
went about doing good and healing all who were
oppressed by the devil, for God was with him. And we
are witnesses of all that he did both in the country of the
Jews and in Jerusalem. They put him to death by
hanging him on a tree, but God raised him on the third
day and made him to appear, not to all the people but to
us who had been chosen by God as witnesses, who ate and
drank with him after he rose from the dead. And he
commanded us to preach to the people and to testify that
he is the one appointed by God to be judge of the living
and the dead. To him all the Prophets bear witness that

everyone <u>who believes in him receives forgiveness of sins through his name.</u>'

What is essential to note in all of these instances is the presence of a covenant relationship. God honours those who honour him, and who through time has developed their trust worthiness with him. Also for those who don't know him, or who know him but despise him He longs for restoration. He disciplines sometimes to bring back to fellowship.

Why does He speak kindly? Why does He hope and anticipate fellowship? Because, He is not a man. The natural tendency of man– in an unredeemed nature, or one not brought under subjection to the spirit of God, is prone to hatred and destructive manipulative tendencies. Understandably, they can't help it. This is why a response must always be one of constant anticipatory decision to forgive. There are also more examples in the bible–

Genesis 37:3-4 tells us – *'Now Israel loved Joseph more than all his sons, because he was the son of his old age; and he made him a varicoloured tunic. His brothers saw that their father loved him more than all his brothers; and <u>so they hated him</u> <u>and could not speak to him on friendly terms.</u>'*

Psalm 120:5-7 David prayed to God about a conflicting situation– *'Woe to me that I dwell in Meshech, that I live among the tents of Kedar! Too long* *have <u>I lived among those who hate peace. I am a man of</u> peace; but when I speak, they are for war.'*

So why can't the carnal mind truly speak good without being deceptive, or even have the humility to acknowledge good? Can we see a human as a human, and nothing demeaning? Would you rather discountenance good, and affirm evil? Jesus Christ puts it this way– our heart's 'actions' precede our physical or outward actions. The heart's devices matter more to God. So what is in your heart? Repentance is changing our heart's call, and subjecting it to the living God. God loves it when despite your imperfections we pursue after perfection, and peace. Peace with God comes by faith in Jesus Christ.

Luke 6:44-45 – *'<u>For each tree is known by its own fruit.</u> For men do not gather figs from thorns, nor do they pick grapes from a briar bush. '<u>The good man out of the good treasure of his heart brings forth what is good</u>; and the evil man out of the evil treasure brings forth what is evil; for his mouth speaks from that which fills his heart.'*

I will show you what to rejoice about. That God's heart is perfect towards you. He speaks highly of you and desire your wellbeing, and that you will walk in every way worthy of Him. You are made in God's image and He wants to see you conform to His image daily. Now go do the same– see others as God sees them, and support them to be all God has called them to be. By first changing you. For the heart would definitely have to precede the lip. See it this way from Philemon Chapter 1, Paul by the help of God's spirit is able to recognise what Christ was doing in Philemon's life and those connected to him, but at the same time encourages him to grasp Christ at work in Onesimus, a steward in his house. It is basically others receiving from the comfort we receive in Christ, letting the grace of God flow. Better still, it is also thanking God for His work in you– encouraging yourself in God, and not being weary but rather counting your blessings. To the Romans, Hebrews, or every nation this word would be relevant. The word is the same, Christ is all that really matters to you and me. Let Christ be seen, it is for our good to rejoice at His revelation. But seriously, can any impede His glorious light?

IX

GOD, AS SOURCE

'For even if there are so-called gods, whether in heaven or on earth (as there are many gods and many lords), <u>yet for us there is one God, the Father, of whom are all things, and we for Him; and one Lord Jesus Christ, through whom are all things, and through whom we live.</u>'~ 1 Corinthians 8:5-6 (NKJV)
'The earth is the Lord's, and <u>everything in it</u>, the world, and all who live in it;' Psalm 24:1 NIV

I thank God for being the source of all things. A narrative of the earth's historical developments, and its sustaining factors I believe is not justly analysed and deeply comprehended without regard to the genuine foundations or 'beginnings' upon which everything else we see here, is based. Brilliant for instance to have processed steel, but my mind also goes to what it is extracted from– iron ore? I am not an expert in these things, but basic knowledge tells us about raw materials. We know raw materials are not made from thin air, and that studying its properties does not explain the source of each composition. If conclusions lead us to 'happen-chances' or series of spontaneous 'bangs' producing intelligent design and structures, then one is right to call such a proposition a 'theory–' which has a level of probability, subject to a better discovery or another impressive theory accounting for the said billions of years. The bible brings in more exactitude– 'God made the heavens and the earth.' How about articulating scientific evidence to explain the dead coming back to life, after three days as in the case of Jesus Christ? And, eye balls made from clay? Even amongst us in this world are those who use dark powers– witchcraft or 'juju,' of whatever name it is called, to invoke spells that defy logic– some deemphasise it by calling this type tricks. But being spiritual, we know that there is spiritual wickedness upon the earth and that there is more to what the human eyes or brain can explain. At some point, the debate should not be if there is a God or gods, but which of these show the true path, and is the LORD– the Almighty? There is definitely the supernatural. Either God should mean something or nothing at all. We should have passed rhetoric. We say– 'God bless' in our greetings, scream 'Jesus Christ!' when in need of help, 'God bless America,' 'God save the Queen (or King),' 'God bless our leaders,' and for unexplainable disasters– we coin the phrase 'acts of God' recognisable in contractual documents as a defence for breach in some jurisdictions, or do I refer to several constitutions including Nigeria's that speaks of a nation 'under God.' Our prayers as individuals or nations are offered to something greater than ourselves– is it possible we haven't truly acknowledged this God we profess? Read this story–

'But there was a man named Simon, who had previously practiced magic in the city and amazed the people of Samaria, saying that he himself was somebody great. They all paid attention to him, from the least to the greatest, saying, 'This man is the power of God that is called Great.' And they paid attention to him because for a long time he had amazed them with his magic. But when they believed Philip as he preached good news about the kingdom of God and the name of Jesus Christ, they were baptized, both men and women. Even Simon himself believed, and after being baptized he continued with Philip. And seeing signs and great miracles performed, he was amazed.' Acts 8:9-13

Simon saw a greater power. It is time to choose where to stand. Also consider this two challenges from Elijah and Joshua—

'Elijah approached all the people and said, 'How long will you hobble back and forth between two opinions? If the Lord is God, follow God. If Baal is God, follow Baal.' The people gave no answer.' 1 Kings 18:21 (CEB)

'But if it seems wrong in your opinion to serve the Lord, then choose today whom you will serve. Choose the gods whom your ancestors served beyond the Euphrates or the gods of the Amorites in whose land you live. But my family and I will serve the Lord.' Joshua 24:15(CEB)

I would like to now restrict the conversation to God as provider of our needs. He provides. He is *'Jehovah Jireh—'* the Lord our provider. He provides for every human being in the world, both good and evil. Because He is a God of love and mercy. Men manipulating wealth from others is a different ball game [and requires taking responsibility rather than accusing God]. The Almighty God, provides. And, for all. Consider this scripture—

'You're familiar with the old written law, 'Love your friend,' and its unwritten companion, 'Hate your enemy.' I'm challenging that. I'm telling you to love your enemies. Let them bring out the best in you, not the worst. When someone gives you a hard time, respond with the energies of prayer, for then you are working out of your true

selves, your God-created selves. This is what God does.
He gives his best—the sun to warm and the rain to
nourish—to everyone, regardless: the good and bad, the
nice and nasty. If all you do is love the lovable, do you
expect a bonus? Anybody can do that. If you simply say
hello to those who greet you, do you expect a medal? Any
run-of-the-mill sinner does that.'   Matthew 5:44-47
(MSG)

To the ancient nation Israel, God said–

'...It's also because the Lord wants to confirm the
promise he swore to your ancestors Abraham, Isaac, and
Jacob. So understand this: It's not because you've been
living right that the Lord your God is giving you this
good land to possess. You are impossible to deal with!'~
Deuteronomy 9:5-6 GWT

There is the law of gravity that keeps things in its
balance upon the earth and does not pick faces, but
responds consistently to all; in the same vein, the
law of seed time and harvest ensures predictability
if the conditions are right, so we benefit from the
earth's resource. As we till our land and plant seeds
gotten from the earth, tending it, it produces a
harvest. By so doing, you and your family have the
opportunity to be fed and refreshed. The soil does
not discriminate on your culture or looks, if the soil
is well taken care of, over the months or years, it

produces a harvest– this is God at work. God provides for us by positioning us to use our God-given resources such as air, water, land, seeds, and minerals in the soil for the enrichment of ourselves and others around us. As we exchange this gift between different groups, each is able to benefit fully from the depth of blessing of His providence. If out of selfishness nations refuse to cooperate, or if the strong oppress the weak and a few become stupendously rich by seizing and blocking access to resource– God should not take the blame. The emphasis is, God provides the resources, but humans act as stewards– intelligent, but usually self-willed, and have been given discretion on its use. God intervenes in hard times when we ask Him for His specific help. Sometimes, without asking, He responds out of His mercy and compassion.

A thought–

'Don't let it escape your notice, dear friends, that with the Lord a single day is like a thousand years and a thousand years are like a single day. The Lord isn't slow to keep his promise, as some think of slowness, but he is patient toward you, not wanting anyone to perish but all to change their hearts and lives.' 2 Peter 3: 8-9

We have seen God providing miraculously; stories are replete in the bible, and there are living testimonies today. He deserves the credit. He could also bring a word to a person or to a nation to preserve them. The same God gifts professionals with skill to empower themselves and serve others, the genuine question is– do they consider His handiwork or think He gave the creativity? The bible tells us of a historical account of the famine in Egypt– warned in a dream prior, Pharaoh asks his counsellors for advice. Joseph a Hebrew immigrant resident in Egypt at that time, inspired by God suggests an economic plan that saved a generation and a nation from extinction. Detailed in the scriptures. It is not unusual to have men even now, called by God and gifted to bring healing to a nation and spiritual guidance. Just like Daniel, Moses, the sons of Issachar, Elisha and so many others. Amazing works they did. Most people in our generation have heard of Billy Graham and several Christian leaders in their nation (known and unknown), who pray for presidents and leaders in high authority. And often challenge them to care for the needs of the poor, and work godly. What I speak of is not strange, if we seek God's guidance we would find it.

This is what God would say to this generation– a reference to 2 Chronicles 20:20.

'The army got up early the next morning and headed out into the wilderness of Tekoa. Jehoshaphat stood up and addressed them. 'Listen to me, you inhabitants of Judah

and Jerusalem,' he said. <u>'Have faith in the LORD your God and you'll be established! Have faith in his prophets and you'll succeed!'</u>

There is a special covenant for those who believe in Jesus Christ, and by faith have come into relationship with God. Their soul find peace in the midst of life's turbulence. God promises to meet their needs, and even if persecution arise to detract, there is the promise of an eternal reward. A life no one can take, a life with Christ. Except the Lord wills otherwise, even in this fleeting life spanning on average almost 70-80years, our God is an unshakeable rock and support. He is faithful and can be trusted. God could provide anything– raw materials, potentials, and even 'finished goods' miraculously. Don't put limits on God. The same God that could inspire someone to send a financial gift, or prompt you to give generously is the same God that can do anything to help. When we give to a cause God approves of, it is not us saying we are all-sufficient rather it is us saying to God– we acknowledge you as the source of all we've got. You gave me the wisdom, the potential, the goods, the power to work, and every reward it brings. This kind of thinking is powerful, because it restructures one's mind to realise the need for thankfulness, fills you with humility and reminds us all, that we at best stewards of the incredible benefit of His provision. The obligation then, is to handle it in a way that best glorifies Him.

X

THE ART AND ACT OF WORSHIP OF THE LIVING GOD

'So tell me, why is it that you Jews insist that Jerusalem is the only place of worship, while we Samaritans claim it is here at Mount Gerizim, where our ancestors worshiped?' Jesus replied, 'Believe me, dear woman, the time is coming when it will no longer matter whether you worship the Father on this mountain or in Jerusalem. You Samaritans know very little about the one you worship, while we Jews know all about him, for salvation comes through the Jews. But the time is coming—indeed it's here now—when true worshipers will worship the Father in spirit and in truth. The Father is looking for those who will worship him that

way. For God is Spirit, so those who worship him must worship in spirit and in truth.' John 4: 20-24.

Worship– is an expression of love and adoration for God, for who He is, what He has done in creation and providence, and in fulfilment of His word. He commands and seeks for it. God loves to take credit for what He has done, He desires worship earnestly from sincere hearts. A few things about worship: where should I worship? Is God, and God alone the object of our worship? How long are we to worship him? To what purpose is worship?

On a visual broadcast via the internet once, I heard a passionate atheist articulate concerns about a God that must be low self-esteem stricken, as He needs seemingly inferior beings to tickle his fancy, to retain a sense of worth. Why should our words affect this so called 'big' and 'sovereign' King or Creator? Well, not to be dismissive, what does it matter if He chooses what to be annoyed at– that still would be sovereignty at work as He can do anything! A parent might choose not to be grieved by his child's bad attitudes towards him, even more unworthy if his actions has been born out of goodwill. If he is grieved it is more likely than not, that he cares deeply.

When we know God and His nature, only then we come to understand Him to the extent the bible lets us into and as He reveals by His Spirit. He is a person, and has made us look like him. He is pure hearted, and claims full credit for all that there is. He also has made Himself known in Jesus Christ. To worship God is to revere Him as righteous and worthy of the honour due to His name. When we obey Him we exercise our reverence for Him, through our life choices, and definitely before we begin thinking astray– this is not a reference to personal worldview or cultural-induced obedience, but bible based belief. Our life then effuses honour for the Most High. Jesus reveals that true worship to and of God, must be birthed from a place of revelation and divine understanding, out of a spirit of gratitude and sincerity. The place of worship becomes periphery in the context of God being the object of our worship, a God who lives in our heart. Our body is the house or temple for the living God, it is His residence, as He lives in us by His spirit. This is true if you trust God's word and believe Jesus Christ is your Lord and personal saviour from all your sins, whether be open and secret sins of the heart or overt life actions.

So, worship is we saying to God, we love you, we thank you, and we adore you. I tell you He gets jealous when we give this level of attention to 'idols' we make. He is a jealous God. There are those who make 'good luck charms' and put their faith in it. Others consult magicians and spiritualists for their business success or to inquire about their future. Some read the signs of stars, moons and sun to understand more about themselves, rather than seeking God through His word. Usually, God is out of the equation– this is an error. Idols or images that capture our complete adoration that exist in our minds, or literal idols made out of physical things or objects in which we hope in as our 'saviour' would all have to be put away, if we want to worship the living God. They can't compete for His place. He is the author of worship– His terms are, He alone is worthy of all worship and that we ought to cleanse our hearts and lives of all things that distract from Him.

Years ago Prophet Jeremiah gave God's message to the nation Israel, calling them back again to true worship and reminding them of the deliverance God gave them when certain nations sought to eliminate them. This word is relevant to all nations and persons that seek to serve God in worship today.

Jeremiah 2:11-13 & 27-29

'Has a nation changed its gods, Which are not gods? But My people have changed their Glory for what does not profit. Be astonished, O heavens, at this, and be horribly afraid; be very desolate,' says the Lord. 'For My people have committed two evils: they have forsaken Me, the

fountain of living waters, and hewn themselves cisterns—broken cisterns that can hold no water.

... Saying to a tree, 'You are my father,' and to a stone, 'You gave birth to me.' For they have turned their back to Me, and not their face. But in the time of their trouble they will say, 'Arise and save us.' But where are your gods that you have made for yourselves? Let them arise, if they can save you in the time of your trouble; for according to the number of your cities are your gods, O Judah. 'Why will you plead with Me? You all have transgressed against Me,' says the Lord.'

God says I formed you with my hands from the dust of the ground, and breathed into you my life, you are not a product of random chance, or from trees or stones. He is saying, give me glory, can't you see? I made you. It is God screaming for attention, saying aloud I deserve worship. It is not God portrayed as an attention seeking maniac, but rather He pinpoints the obnoxious tendency to ignore the obvious and not relinquishing 'control' to Him, even though He could conform us robotically to do so if He wanted. This precisely, He says is the sin of our generation, turning away from Him. The joy of God is to see all nations worship at His feet, and actually it is a pleasure to worship God. He deserves it and is worthy of it. It is not a rule-driven, it is heart-birthed.

Psalms 33:4-12 message bible says it like this—

'For God's Word is solid to the core; everything he makes is sound inside and out. He loves it when everything fits, when his world is in plumb-line true. Earth is drenched in God's affectionate satisfaction. The skies were made by God's command; he breathed the word and the stars popped out. He scooped Sea into his jug, put Ocean in his keg.

Earth-creatures, bow before God; world-dwellers—down on your knees! Here's why: he spoke and there it was, in place the moment he said so. God takes the wind out of Babel pretense, he shoots down the world's power-schemes. God's plan for the world stands up, all his designs are made to last. Blessed is the country with God for God; blessed are the people he's put in his will.'

Worship must be freely given from the heart, no one can be compelled to. True worship focuses on Jesus Christ. On Jesus Christ's birth, the bible tells us wise men came and worshipped Him, they also brought gifts as an act of reverence for Him. Worship was not the gifts, but the expression of faith. Worship is saying with all of our body and life as well as the fruit of it, that God we honour you as God. There ought to be a correlation, simultaneous affirmation of everything within us that we love and honour God. The fruit of the lip ought to be in tandem with the ministration of the heart. The size of our offering would not matter, if the heart's worship is not right before God. If we dance before God as an act in His honour and truly in our heart we honour Him as God, then our worship glorifies Him. If our words truly adore Him, then He is pleased. If we decide even not to speak, but quietly glorify Him, He also takes glory. When we believe, then we speak. Worship is the overflow of our heart's worship. The beauty is in the synergy and the motive. Humility lubricates the engines of worship, it opens up one's heart to accept our smallness in light of His awesome greatness. It becomes less of the opinions about you, or the lack of attention whilst in secret, but all about the greatness of Him.

Worship is always of faith. The story of Abel and Cain as illustrated in the bible offers a very insightful lesson. Abel's offering was acceptable over Cain's because he honoured God in it. He believed God. Same, for father Abraham– his belief in God became the justifiable act of righteousness. Others acted, perhaps even more 'practically,' but it was void not being of faith. Actions do not birth worship, but worship in faith produces action and fruit acceptable to God. Jesus reference to a widow's little giving exceeding that of the Pharisees who literally gave more becomes instructive. Or do we speak of His word to Martha and Mary- in essence, He esteemed more highly the act of seating at his feet to listen over preparing a home to make Him comfy. This is to be balanced alongside God's pleasure over the abundance of King Solomon's giving. It is not the size or actions in worship, it is the right heart of worship. Not even to despise another in our heart as they worship God. There must be a genuine belief that God is worthy of all glory, and able to keep His word; our hearts must glorify Him as God. Whether we decide to walk about and praise Him in worship, or sit, or dance, or speak of His greatness in adoration, or bless Him with the fruit of our body, or be in silence— our worship must flow from a heart that is connected to Him as revealed in Jesus Christ, and sincerely glorify Him as God. From this standpoint we can effectively do the others. Being on God's side in our art of worship is the act needed.

XI

ALIGNING WITH THE KING OF THE UNIVERSE

This happened in order to make come true what the prophet had said: 'Tell the city of Zion, look, your king is coming to you! He is humble and rides on a donkey and on a colt, the foal of a donkey.' Matthew 21:4-5

This fulfilled the prophecy of Jeremiah that says, 'They took the thirty pieces of silver—the price at which he was valued by the people of Israel, and purchased the potter's field, as the Lord directed.' Now Jesus was standing before Pilate, the Roman governor. 'Are you the king of the Jews?' the governor asked him. Jesus replied, 'You have said it.' Matthew 27:9:11

Is there such a King? Who is He? – Jesus Christ. He is not only the King of Kings, He is creator God, of both the inhabitants of the world and grants authorisation of its systems, and He is in complete control. He promises to reconcile all things in the 'fullness of time.' I tell you [people], the Kingdom of God is a spiritual Kingdom not made with human hands, yet its operation supersedes any on the earth put together. God's purpose is that His will as operational in Heaven be manifested upon the affairs of the earth. You may ask how practical this is– the bible is the compass, it points to what the detailed will of the King is. This is the will of God- that you return to Him your creator and acknowledge His reign, and yield your life to him. It is like a father beckoning on his child to understand and receive unconditionally His love. This knowledge puts us in perspective, we stop seeing ourselves as the final arbiter of our lives, but in total humility we recognise that we are only a fragment in human existence, and that truly we owe our gratitude to the one greater and mightier than us.

When you believe in what God has done in Jesus Christ, you come into alignment, into a heavenly purpose. You come into divine royalty, what can be greater? What a priviledge! This is not a futuristic obtuse desire, I mean now. [To the believer] Now, you are a son of God. Now, you are by faith a partaker of His nature. Now, you are heir of God's blessings. Now, you are in position with Christ. When we see Him finally, the bible tells us there is greatness planned which would be revealed, but what has been revealed already calls for rejoicing. That we, any, has been found worthy, in this life to have a relationship with King Jesus Christ. If you knew Him, nothing, absolute nothing compares to this glory. Both great and small are invited at this table. Known and unknown are welcome. Those even with fleeting riches are invited. Oh that we know Him, and pray that He would grant us the priviledge to peep daily, more and more into the revelation of His grace.

1 Peter 2:9 *'But you are a chosen race, a royal priesthood, a dedicated nation, [God's] own purchased, special people, that you may set forth the wonderful deeds and display the virtues and perfections of Him Who called you out of darkness into His marvellous light.'*

Revelation 1:4-6 says, *'Grace to you and peace from Him who is and who was and who is to come, and from the seven Spirits who are before His throne, and from Jesus Christ, the faithful witness, the firstborn from the dead, and the ruler over the kings of the earth. To Him who loved us and washed us from our sins in His own blood, and has made us kings and priests to His God and Father, to Him be glory and dominion forever and ever. Amen.'*

God has made us royalty– 'kings and priests' to God, for those who believe in Jesus Christ and what He has done. As a sign, Jesus was born into the King David's messianic lineage as prophesied years before, and He affirmed it while He walked the earth. Another proof for you is that while hundreds and thousands of prophets are dead, King Jesus Christ still lives, the grave could not keep Him. He is the author and finisher of life and of our faith– the Alpha and Omega. This is the Jesus Christ, I preach. Not a fairy-tale baby kept for Christmas, or an Easter egg or bunny, no. May nothing erode His essence– He is more than that [annual celebratory figure], I mean your King. You don't have to compulsorily accept Him, as it doesn't change His status, however, it is for your good and joy to come into alignment with Him and accept Him as your Lord and saviour from sins. He wishes you do. As surely as the principle of sowing and reaping, He promises to bring all deeds to account, of every person. Beyond the world's system that show favouritism, we really should worry about Him. If you come under His forgiveness and righteousness, you will be saved, this is the good news of the cross. (Acts 4:12) Your King and my King, He is Lord of all the earth. Every believer comes under His reign, and He has made us kings. What a glorious God.

XII

YOU ARE OF INCREDIBLE VALUE TO GOD: GOD'S PERSPECTIVE ON LIFE

Matthew 10: 29-31.

'Aren't two sparrows sold for a penny? Not one of them will fall to the ground without your Father's permission. Every hair on your head has been counted. Don't be afraid! You are worth more than many sparrows.'

Psalms 139: 13- 17

'You made my whole being; you formed me in my mother's body. I praise you because you made me in an amazing and wonderful way. What you have done is wonderful. I know this very well. You saw my bones

being formed as I took shape in my mother's body. When I was put together there, you saw my body as it was formed. All the days planned for me were written in your book before I was one day old. God, your thoughts are precious to me. They are so many!'

The person of God for some might be perplexing and even troubling, but it need not be. If we insist on sight to always ascertain the reality of God, we miss it, just as 'air,' it breezes past us. I begin from the premise that the truth of His existence is ingrained in the very fabric of the human heart– a knowledge that all there is transcends the physical realm. The bible, yes, is a prophetic book of future occurrences, but also of detailed incidences that men of old have classed as acts done by supernatural influence– the parting of the Red Sea, victories in warfare by feeble nations, miraculous healings that beat human imaginations, and words of life as spoken by many of God's servants that bring healing to nations and families. And because believers of God, serve a living God, God's word as contained in the bible is true for today and proves itself– no prop ups needed.

One of the vital truth the bible points to, is the value God places on His creation. We assume rightly and need not dispute certain artificial things have a manufacturer or creator– car, house, technology, but humans, some contemplate as a creation of random chance; there you go. All of God's created work, reveals a dimension of His glory. To disprove God's label, try creating something from nothing, that includes not even using one's self as a start point or resource. That's inconceivable. Man as a design is a master piece, made by an intelligent God. He places huge value on what His hands have formed, with such incredible detail and complexity, in His likeness– a prototype of Himself, though corrupted by sin the bible tells us he has a 'restore point' in Christ Jesus. Why? Because He loves us, so we can function in our full capacity. From the beginning it was not His ordination to have a world filled with such evil or pain, but sin (birthed by a disregard of God and His commands) has infiltrated and brought with it disastrous repercussions. Now, a loving God has to balance His 'justice nature' with the covenant of His love. Love, for Him is also justice, the bible tells us of cases where He has exerted that. He promises eternal judgment for all sin– eternal damnation, there is however, redemption and forgiveness in Christ, as He has paid the punishment of sin on the cross. So instead of eternal separation from Him and torment as Jesus suggested, there is a sure hope of everlasting life in Him.

Jeremiah 1:5 and Isaiah 43:1 shows us of a loving God that knows us by name, even before we gained any knowledge of Him. As Jesus Christ says, God takes notice even of the minutest detail of the hair on our head! What manner of God is so great, yet so intimate? Well, Jesus said this and I believe Him. No one knows the father better than Him, as He is the representation of the invisible father– His express image. God places a high premium on the human life, as He made the earth's substance for our nourishment. He promises to judge evil, but waits patiently so those who do evil might turn from their ways and be saved too by believing in Him. This is the story of God's grace, a time comes when it will be late. In fact, His radical wish is that none would perish under His final wrath to come, being a God of love. He does not adjust the truth but provide a way of escape. The believer has received His nature, and daily growing into His character, to show kindness not because of timidity but a hope for a turnaround in the hearts of those who scheme evil. A time comes when God changes the tune.

Finally, it is important to know that His love for those who believe in His name, is boundless. He promises to protect and defend them, for the reputation of His name. A good example is the nation of Israel, of God's unfailing power towards them anytime they depend on Him. This is true for every nation or persons, who hope in Jehovah God. They would not be confounded.

'But blessed is the one who trusts in the Lord, whose confidence is in him. They will be like a tree planted by the water that sends out its roots by the stream. It does not fear when heat comes; its leaves are always green. It has no worries in a year of drought and never fails to bear fruit.'

Jeremiah 17:7-8

I thought it well to let you know, you are of incredible value to God. You cannot be measured by any monetary value in this world, even to the measure of trillions of whatever. If that amount cannot create life, or bring back the dead, then that it is not worth your value. You cost Christ His blood. Think of that. May nothing, make you feel underserving of His love, burst through the cloud of your thoughts and embrace the truth Christ offers.

XIII

THE CROSS: MAN'S ENVY, GOD'S LOVE!

'Who is wise and understanding among you? Let them show it by their good life, by deeds done in the humility that comes from wisdom. But if you harbour bitter envy and selfish ambition in your hearts, do not boast about it or deny the truth. Such 'wisdom' does not come down from heaven but is earthly, unspiritual, and demonic. For where you have envy and selfish ambition, there you find disorder and every evil practice. But the wisdom that comes from heaven is first of all pure; then peace-loving, considerate, submissive, full of mercy and good fruit, impartial and sincere. Peacemakers who sow in peace

reap a harvest of righteousness.' James 3:13-18 (Mark 15:10)

This is a hard word, but necessary. The grace of God is to reveal the dangers of a vice and a way of escape, found in only Christ and not ourselves. So why does God detest envy passionately? What does the cross of Jesus Christ offer? Envy, is to look at another and what they have with disdain, jealousy, or a sense of 'I deserve that, I could be better–' a covetous and pride-stricken spirit. More disturbing is if the person in this bondage cannot see or count how blessed too they are, as ingratitude drives them to hate another, fulfilling a 'Nathan parable.' Lucifer was dethroned as he considered God's majesty and thought of a takeover, again if he knew Christ would resurrect back to life and make many righteous through His sacrifice, he would not have plotted his 'downfall' at first. To envy has no real pay as when it comes full circle the reward is spiritual death, a lack of accomplishment because of the futility and emptiness, and loops of betrayals it engenders. You might not recall the moments, but a forceful rethink will excavate the tensions and folly in desiring another person's belongings at any expense, or where it means stepping back to gain passively from another's mischievous acts. Envy, discredits others' success for no reason. It refuses to compliment or acknowledge a specific progress, it generalises or trivialise to suppress and control. It assumes you have not attained what you have attained so to keep you in servitude. It lies or furthers a 'no-evidence based idea' to just make a point or injure for self-pride sake. A demonic envious spirit would rather destroy everything than let a person entitled to, have it, as it does not bring any direct or indirect benefit to him or others he thinks should have it. This thinking cannot envisage giving with no strings. It is similar to murder. There is every evil work. This spirit sees truth but refuses its reign. It holds it in unrighteousness, it is not blind but fears the triumph of truth. It chooses to belittle another even if it sees a matter or person is set in a large place. It is a complete loss of objectivity or authenticity. This spirit works to assume no such thing as uniqueness for the object of hate, so finds a gap to excuse originality because of the fear of something else taking precedence, apart from it. This habit will never endorse another as better even when glaring. For humility can esteem another better when due even at risk of personal pride. Envy denies wisdom, it brands it vain. The whole goal is self-preservation. At the end envy destroys itself from within its own archives as it rejects help when it should, enthrones the ignorant, endorses folly to make a point, traps the innocent, excludes what is essential, then before it knows it has robed itself for 'temporary non-lasting pleasure' and sense of accomplishment. Bit by bit these structures built with human minds and held by deep-deep level deception shifts and ebbs away. You can't hold an idea preserved by terror.

This is where God comes in. He says let your heart flow love, justice for the poor and rich, rules not 'face-penned' one of unswerving application, let everyone have their due, let merry hearts sing, let dreamers dream, let liberty be at the expense of one's own responsibility not another man's [forced against his will], and hope cherished. Let's not be fooled, as these things cannot be in isolation from the source of all things– Jesus Christ. This I believe, according to the enduring word of God. For He empowers true love, where martyrs die for a worthy cause and for another, not for selfish interest– whether be for now or in a later life, but for love and worthy conviction. He empowers love where the poor are served not to gain a political 'seat,' or setup an opportunity to 'profile' for investigative purpose, or build up a 'philanthropic cv' but for the promptings of a compassionate spirit. He empowers love where talents and skills are not for trapping the ignorant but supporting the weak. These principles are 'anathemas' to the un-renewed soul, and a human spirit not alive in Christ. What Christ offers is a spiritual heart transplant, the gentle nurture, and constant cultivation of His word. This is what the cross of Calvary on which

He died a death He did not deserve symbolise, as the sinless Lord identifies with the deadness of the human spirit, but by His resurrection to life offers redemption to all who believe in Him. For by faith in Him we have newness of life. Only then this grip of envy and all its evil work can be broken. No replacement methodology can suppress Christ's finished work. The wicked can seek to overwhelm any goodness by covering it with a lie or a chosen 'name,' but not the name above all names, so the one who has real knowledge is not envious of the wicked or foolish person because He knows their end. As God is the ultimate judge, lets' see how we encourage each other to follow what is righteous and rely on Christ. This is only a part of the plagues of sin the human heart can be susceptible to, but in all, Christ still remains the answer, as He clothes the believer in His accomplishment on the Cross, not the strength of our effort. No man is then justified by attempting to be perfect without Christ, because the best effort is 'filthy rags' without the blood washed 'garments' be bestows. The love of God is seen in this gift, of which the charge is to stay spotless of every guile with the strength again He supplies. He is Alpha and Omega, He initiates and concludes. 'For whosoever shall keep the whole law and yet offend on one point, he is guilty of all-' James 2:10, but thank God for Galatians 2:16, which declares that no one is justified in observing the laws, because no one can truly keep it. The way is turning from the dogmas, to relationship in Christ only then this God-life will naturally flow out of you. Each day as you rely on Christ you will grow and become like Him. This is the only real chance of pleasing God, as human will, or a false sense of good life clearly do not cut it. I know, I am sure you agree. Simply, Jesus Christ is the way and solution.

XIV

GOD HAS GOT LOOKS

Sometime ago my heart meditated on what God looks like, and the relevance of that to a believer of Jesus Christ. God is a Spirit man, so cannot be trapped or limited to a physical attribute. The bible tells us we are made in His image, so we take His form [as believers of Christ, as our spirit being in us is alive to God, not dead, so we can perceive spiritual things, which the world can't]. He is also a 'consuming fire,' and sovereign Lord, we also take His form as 'flames of fire' in the spirit realm, and His beloved Angels (powerful spiritual beings) minister to us in protection and godly service. Since no man has seen God in His fullness we have to access Him by faith. By faith, I believe He has revealed Himself in Jesus Christ (John 1:18-19), and that any who really wants to know Him can do so. In Christ we cannot only behold His glory as we peep into the word, but understand that like the early Apostles can touch, handle that which is precious and lay at His bosom. He is the image of the father, indeed if we see Him we have seen the father. Two scriptures I just want to highlight that points to Him. But first beyond His looks we ought to be in reverence, awe of His greatness and holy fear of His person. Our visualisation of Him as a harmless cute man (He is, but more, being the lamb of God– for sacrifice for remission of sins), or baby in a manger (He was, but now the High Priest making intercession for the saints), or nice gentleman in a suit in heaven, must shift (He is rather the Lion of the tribe of Judah, the messiah as promised). The resurrected Christ is lovely, but also we must understand none can stand the strength of His power and glory. This helps us love Him, as then we can understand the magnitude of His power tamed by the gentility and forcefulness of His love. The scriptures for meditation are found in Revelations, Chapter 1, and 19. (One could also consider Christ appearing to Saul of Tarsus in the brightness of His light, and His appearing to the Apostles on resurrection– eating with them, and unrestrained by physical elements as He visits them and later is lifted up to the clouds).

The first excerpt from chapter one of Revelation gives us a partial glimpse to the reality of His person–

In verses 10-18 Apostle John in a revelation saw Christ in a measure of his glory– *'On the Lord's Day I was in the Spirit, and I heard behind me a loud voice like a trumpet, which said: 'Write on a scroll what you see and send it to the seven churches: to Ephesus, Smyrna, Pergamum, Thyatira, Sardis, Philadelphia and Laodicea.' I turned around to see the voice that was speaking to me. And when I turned I saw seven golden lampstands, and among the lampstands was someone like a son of man, dressed in a robe reaching down to his feet and with a golden sash around his chest. The hair on his head was white like wool, as white as snow, and his eyes were like blazing fire. His feet were like bronze glowing in a furnace, and his voice was like the sound of rushing waters. In his right hand he held seven stars, and coming out of his mouth was a sharp, double-edged sword. His face was like the sun shining in all its brilliance. When I saw him, I fell at his feet as though dead. Then he placed his right hand on me and said: 'Do not be afraid. I am the First and the Last. I am the Living One; I was dead, and now look, I am alive for ever and ever! And I hold the keys of death and Hades.'*

The second excerpt:

Again, see verses 11- 16 *'I saw heaven standing open and there before me was a white horse, whose rider is called Faithful and True. With justice he judges and wages war. His eyes are like blazing fire, and on his head are many crowns. He has a name written on him that no one knows but he himself. He is dressed in a robe dipped in blood, and his name is the Word of God. The armies of heaven were following him, riding on white horses and dressed in fine linen, white and clean. Coming out of his mouth is a sharp sword with which to strike down the nations. 'He will rule them with an iron scepter.' He treads the winepress of the fury of the wrath of God Almighty. On his robe and on his thigh he has this name written: king of kings and lord of lords.'*

An oil painting of this description will be humbling– I would imagine, and like to have. How much more seeing Him face to face. When God parted the red sea, or later on in the 'exodus journey' descended on Sinai in thunder and dark clouds to the children of Israel, or as a flaming fire in the bush to Moses, or to Elijah in a whisper in the wind– one thing is clear is His greatness. We can't pick a form we prefer but we can worship at His greatness and humility as revealed. Also, let's consider how we receive of this grace and understanding for restraint and love, as we love a God we cannot see now until we meet Him [face to face], to love those we can see now. I will leave you with the most important scripture of all in relation to this– I John 4:20-21, *'If anyone says, 'I love God,' and hates his brother, he is a liar; for he who does not love his brother whom he has seen cannot love God whom he has not seen. And this commandment we have from him: whoever loves God must also love his brother.'*

XV

GOD IS REVEALED IN CHRIST:

THE PERSON OF JESUS, SOME SPECIFIC POINTS IN SCRIPTURE TO CONSIDER

a. When Jesus Christ was born He was esteemed worthy of worship. We are made and born to worship Him. Consider this scripture in Matthew 2:2, the wise men came to worship Christ as God. '*...we saw his star in the east and have come to worship him-*' Matthew 2:2.

b. Knowing Jesus Christ, is believing in your heart what He says of Himself, that He is Lord and saviour. Just as the scriptures say. It is more than a head knowledge, it requires a sincere belief in your heart, John 8:53-56; 5:19-47.

c. *'He was chosen before the creation of the world, but was revealed in these last times for your sake-'* 1 Peter 1:20 (NIV). Jesus Christ pre-existed the universe. His birth on earth wasn't the beginning of life for Him, as you may be told. And He is actually the source of all things.

d. For in Christ there is all of God in a human body, Colossians 2:9 (LB).

e. King Herod who reigned at the time of Christ's birth requested the wise men to find baby Jesus and bring him word so he too can worship. However, his real intent was to destroy (as though he could have)- Matthew 2:1-12. This meaning, not all who seek to worship, really mean to. Do you intend to know God, or are you fishing for religion to identify with? Christ promises to be known to the one who is yearning for God, the source of all life.

f. Literally, God came down to live with humanity.

The Word (Jesus Christ) became flesh and blood,
and moved into the neighbourhood.
We saw the glory with our own eyes,
the one-of-a-kind glory,
like Father, like Son,
Generous inside and out,
true from start to finish. John 1:14 MSG

g. Several scriptural prophecies preceding Jesus' birth are worthy of reference. If He is the Christ and messiah (that is, the one who ultimately deals with evil in the world and restores God to man, as He is) then Jesus will have to fulfil every one of those prophecies– no coincidences (which He did). A few– He would have to be born of a virgin in Bethlehem but raised in Nazareth, come from the lineage of King David, receive the affirmation of God by mighty miracles and signs, live a sinless life, become a sacrifice for sin by dying a criminal's death of Roman crucifixion, also to be buried but rise from the dead after 3 days. He is to live forever and raise a people to himself from all nations. This is the Jesus we preach. The fulfilment of this narrative is shown in the scriptures, and I believe proves Jesus is the Christ, the son of the living God. Any who attempts to impersonate the Christ would have to tick all these boxes and be set in the time of the prophecy specified. Incredible Christ fulfilled these things, and leaves for us an example. This is why this man Jesus is worthy of having a closer look and meticulous enquiry about. See John 6:45; Matthew 26:56.

h. Man is on an endless search for the truth of God, and His plan for humanity. Jesus Christ revealed why He came to the earth, testified to the truth of God's unfailing love for mankind, and unveiled His redemptive plan. He said, *'For this cause I was born, and for this cause I have come into the world, that I should bear witness to the truth-'* John 18:37 (NKJV).

i.   Friends, this Jesus, is not only a 'witness to the truth,' but is the 'truth.' How can this be? This is because He bears witness of Himself, yet His testimony is true! (John 8:13-20) He is the way, the truth and life. I pray when you meet Him, that you will have the revelation of the truth. You meet Him by His word (scriptures). Pilate before the truth asked, 'what is the truth?,' John the Baptist however screamed, 'Behold the Lamb of God that takes the sins of the world.' Hope you see this truth– and have a recognition. The Spirit of God takes the word we preach, and transforms a life. No human being can have a true revelation of Jesus Christ, except the Spirit of God reveals Him. To some He was a Carpenter's son, to others, 'Rabbi' meaning teacher. The truth however is, He is Christ the Lord. For God became flesh and dwelt among men. His name *Emmanuel* means, God with us! May the Holy Spirit in every season reveal Jesus Christ, as Lord to you. 1 Corinthians 12:3, *'... and no one can say, 'Jesus is Lord,' except by the Holy Spirit.'*

j.   *'Without faith no one can please God. Anyone who comes to God must believe that he is real and that he rewards those who truly want to find him-'* Hebrews 11:6 (NCV). From the scriptures, God actually expects the agnostic or atheist to sincerely search for Him, with their hearts open. He promises to be found– no longer hidden. The truth is, the bible provides the road map. Christ's desire to be found, is far greater than our desire to find Him. It begins with a step of faith. Faith, His words are true. Faith in Him.

k. Jesus Christ is the Light of the world. He reveals God the father, to humanity! John 8: 12– '...*I am the light of the world. Whoever follows me will never walk in darkness, but will have the light of life.*'

XVI

ON CONTENTMENT:

YOUR TRUEST SATISFACTION IS IN CHRIST

John 4:13-14 says,

'Jesus answered and said to her, 'whoever drinks of this water will thirst again, but whoever drinks of the water that I shall give him will never thirst. But the water that I shall give him will become in him a fountain of water springing up into everlasting life.'

I think contentment is linked with thankfulness and discerning the purpose of God in your life. In this age of technologically driven advancement, and a plethora of consumerist ideas and materialistic choices, what could come to the forefront or bubbleup is the desperation of one's situation, fuelled by a sense of unmet desires. What would not have mattered before, now does. Now you can see your friend or enemy has a peculiar advantage compared to yours– which could either be depressing or really sensational and an inspiration. How you deal with this kind of 21st century pressure is crucial. First, I suggest you look inwards and outwards of your life and do what I call a 'decisive journey checklist,' to find areas you can be thankful for in your walk. You have to do so, so you keep the right perspective. You are only at pace with your own goals, not another's. And of course, your experiences are noteworthy, we are not all dealt the same lot. We all have diverse challenges, in fact some persons may not survive five minutes in your world, vice versa may be true. So pause and say, God thank you for this, and that, and for all you have planned for the future. In your life's journey you have had doubtlessly grilling moments but also joys– yeah? So, if you don't make the effort to share, reflect on, or celebrate your progress, no one else will do like you do, because no one else can tell your story with the same depth of gratitude– because you see, only you know how you managed through it. I also suggest you begin to recognise God was often the unseen hand helping you through difficult times. I encourage you to consider God's plans for you as revealed in the bible, as He wants you to live in a manner that give Him the best glory. Evil doing will not glorify God, only trusting Christ will. Ask God for the grace to be grateful and contented for all He has done for you, as you reach for all He has for you, only within His will. The truest blessings that exceeds all others comes from what Jesus Christ can give. I challenge you to go for Christ Himself. For in coming into relationship with Christ, it will not matter life circumstances, because you have the greatest treasure. He is the water that won't run dry.

PART II: THE GOSPEL OF JESUS CHRIST

XVII

GOD'S MASTER PLAN OF SALVATION FOR THE NATIONS

Of salvation through Jesus Christ of Nazareth alone, not through any other religion or any unique denomination, system or institution.

I strongly recommend reading the scriptures thoroughly to grasp the purpose of God, and to check if any teaching you hear is true. Also, I suggest to persons seeking to understand the gospel, and new believers to seek fellowship with other Christians, and consider an in-depth study of the foundational doctrine of salvation, especially as espoused by the Evangelical, Charismatic and Pentecostal community, where they lay right emphasis on the work of Christ for redemption from sin and the full work of the Holy Spirit today and the manifestation of His gifts. Also as well as with any group or person that do same. My hope is to see that Christ is preached.

As Apostle Paul stood in Mars Hill articulating his faith in Christ, so I pray I am able to communicate to you by all means necessary, whether online, via this book medium, or by speech when in your presence, by the grace of God. Intellectually with all emotion, prayerfully in all spiritual wisdom and knowledge, and using all the gifts the Holy Spirit has graced me with according to my ability– so you will be convinced that Christ is Lord. None of my abilities matter if not empowered by the Spirit, and no compelling of the Spirit matter if you will not receive the word, even Christ could do no mighty work where there was unbelief. He didn't express disappointment at His inability, or whether they were programmed or configure not to obey; He was just astonished at their unbelief, their resistance to the Spirit.

I believe the Lord is slow and patient with you to come to faith, even you, don't mess it up. None of us deserves this grace, and all who believe are forever reliant on the grace of Jesus Christ, from the beginning of our walk to the end of it! I pray the Lord who granted me this opportunity, the will and power to communicate this truth, will *impress on you to open your heart and hear the beckoning of the Spirit today, whilst you have time in this life.*

XVIII

WHAT THE WORD OF GOD CAUSES

There is power in the living word of God. The word of God could redirect lives, wash clean from any ideology that misinterprets the person of God. The proper food for the human soul is from the very breathe of God, His Spirit word, that quickens the spiritually dead. What has been infused in my Spirit to share with you, is about the nature of this commitment to the word. Satan dreads the word of God, so he attacks it even though the fruit is admirable and life giving. Persecution arises for the word's sake. The answer is not to stop the flow of the word into your Spirit, but to make sure that this life and the elements of it don't choke you. The enemy will always attack you, not because of you, but for it– Mark 4:17 says, 'And have no root in themselves, and so endure but for a time: afterward, when affliction or persecution ariseth for the word's sake, immediately they are offended.' You could read the context of this parable on the sower who sows good seeds, and each circumstance determines the result we see. But I will focus not so much on how receptive the heart is to the word, the rootedness of the word, or on figuratively the 'thorns,' that is, life's conflict and temptation that may choke the word– rather, that the word brings a level of attack we need to be aware of. Of course– nonetheless, this explains why one needs rootedness, and the right conditions for the word to be fruitful, but don't be naïve of the device of the enemy to frustrate the word and to steal it, that is, hindering its effectiveness. To think the word will make all things nice and lovely, with harmless sumptuous plants springing around you is naïve, alright, and not the truth, many are offended because they think the word or identifying with Christ should see their troubles abate naturally. That is focusing on the wrong mind-set, you should pray for rootedness so when life's snares come, you are firm. And be aware that though the word brings victory and triumph, but also persecution. (Philippians 1:29; 2 Timothy 3:12).

It's the word that can change you to be who God has called you to be. You don't avoid the word because you don't want to feed on it or speak about it. If you do this I assure you, you will not share in Christ's sufferings, just the decay of the word in your life. You don't want to mix the word with your philosophy or traditions and make it ineffective, Jesus said you cannot mix old and new wine. Basically, if Christ says a matter is fine, you don't say the tradition of my fathers say otherwise. Christ is the true word from heaven. In sharing in His testimony we overcome. Is it not a priviledge to share in Christ's difficulties in any small way? The same word that attracts persecution (however subtle, by this I don't mean only just cases of martyrs in some nations resulting in death, but forms of exclusion, betrayers, mockery, any form of invented pain for the sake of the cross) also brings rejoicing, that the righteous by faith has been counted worthy in whatever scale to serve the purpose of Christ. Nothing must stiffen the growth of the word, keep planting on good soil, deepening your roots, and focus on Christ. The disciples of Christ not only preached the word that brought salvation, but kept at it, till the word produced results and outgrew their circumstances. Ministry is not about building structures, which can be a good thing and important, it is essentially more releasing the word and praying it is not hindered, that it has free course and produce life to the hearers, wherever. Apostle Paul's letters has edified many over the centuries, Christ cannot be bound. Friendship clubs are great, but it is the fellowship of the Spirit through the meditation of the word that will set God's holy fire in our hearts until we are totally conformed to His person. Refuse to not let the word not profit you, by concentrating on the cares and schemes of this life, rather than sharing in the joys of the word, with Christ's suffering, in order to see His power and glory. This is good, and a priviledge if you put your trust in Christ and settle for His word– this understanding shared above will give you strength and comfort, in the storm, because you have the word in you. So your response is understanding the enemy of your faith fights you not just for you but for your faith in the word, the best way forward can only be to advance further in the word. So prepare your heart, protect the word you receive and let it minister to you richly, in depth. For the word of God is greatly priced. Nothing is wrong with the word of God, as it produces life, but Satan attacks you for the word's sake, so you will not be free and enjoy God's salvation. Hebrews 4:12-14 – *'For the word of God is quick, and powerful, and sharper than any two-edged sword, piercing even to the dividing asunder of soul and spirit, and of the joints and marrow, and is a discerner of the thoughts and intents of the heart. Neither is there any creature that is not manifest in his sight: but all things are naked and opened unto the eyes of him with whom we have to do. Seeing then that we have a great high priest, that is passed into the heavens, Jesus the Son of God, let us hold fast our profession.'*

XIX

HOW TO SAVE YOUR SOUL AND SECURE YOUR ETERNAL DESTINY.

An Evangelical note for you

Search the Bible and discover God for yourself. For God loves you, and proved it in Jesus Christ! Everyone, anyone, who comes to Him in prayer, asking Him to save their soul, and confess whatever sin to Him He hears and cleanses. Before God you cannot be good enough, or perfect by your ability so cannot be exempted when before a God of justice, from all your wrongdoing since your moment of rational capacity, even conception. So, Christ who took the full punishment for sin, being blameless yet crucified for sin can be the only substitute. That Christ who historically walked this earth, with the testimony of being God's son, was proved by God, when He bore him witness in mighty miracles, healings and raising him from the dead. And that you must confess Him as your Lord and invite Him into your heart by faith (believing though you don't see Him), and asking Him to save you. You must receive the gift of His suffering for salvation, for your eternal redemption. The earth functions in God ordained laws— day and night, seed-time and harvest-time, birth and death- surely in the same vein all good deeds and evil deeds will be rewarded ultimately in the life to come, and all who qualify as righteous by putting their faith in God's provision for perfection and acceptance would escape a wrath to come. This is the good news, that I didn't meet the standard, but Jesus Christ did, and by trusting him I am saved! When you do this a supernatural work occurs, beyond the human eyes and senses. You then are changed, the spirit being in you comes alive and your relationship with God your heavenly father and creator, restored. You then will be sure that you will be spending eternity with Him. No more doubts or guesses of what lies afterwards. The love of God will be ever present to help you navigate life's greatest battles till we see this glorious Jesus that once walked the face of the earth, face to face!

Reigning in glory as King and Lord, for He is even now. Amen.

XX

FAITH IN THE LOVE OF GOD

Love and faith is connected. Love births faith, faith sustains love. Often, we learn have faith in God, which I believe is a core of the Christian discipline; but recognise there is an ambit to this that buttresses the work of divine grace and understanding, which is to have faith in the love of God. Faith in God is faith in His love, rarely do one have faith in the outrageous and unsurpassed love without a knowledge of God's person. To know God cares, to God protects, to know God meets every need and can do anything, so therefore my trust or faith is in God. And then to in obedience receive Christ, and humbly come to an ever-increasing knowledge of God's love. As a believer I have faith in the love of God, I have faith in God. As God is love, bound to His person is perfect and divine love, inextricably linked, so our faith in Him mirrors His love; our love for God, His supernatural love for us. Also, our expression of genuine faith in God is our standard of love for others who are our neighbours as we do ourselves, with the grace only God can give.

May God help us all through faith in Christ demonstrate continually a love of God that is heavenly. Why live in our own wisdom and not take to heart the unfathomed possibilities that exists if we were to trust Him? If not saved, that is come to believe God yet, today is the day of salvation to first receive Christ's love and then to demonstrate His love. Amen. Now let's meditate on God's word– the love God has for us is the overcoming love.
1 John 4:7-9

'Dear friends, let us continue to love one another, for love comes from God. Anyone who loves is a child of God and knows God. But anyone who does not love does not know God, for God is love. God showed how much he loved us by sending his one and only Son into the world so that we might have eternal life through him.'

Assurance in the love of God:

I am convinced God takes great consideration to our needs being met, both to those of no means or those considerably well off. We see this in the sending of ravens to Elijah story, in the multiplying of the loaves of bread and fishes to feed his disciples, in inspiring the early Church to manage resources towards caretakering for the weak amongst them, even that God sends earth's blessings to support the nourishing of all whether good or evil. I perceive God is equipping us to enable structures and institutions that support well-being. Let God fill you with the assurance that faith brings whether your issues seems main or infinitesimal. Christ is in control and will see to your deepest prayers being met.

XXI

GOD'S WORD:

On the ministry of the word

The ministry of the word prospers wherever it is sent. The physical body may not move but if the word is sent from the body of that regenerated soul in Christ, it operates to mightily bring spiritual succour, to where it is openly received. Where a word is spoken without the Spirit it is void and ineffectual to bring spiritual transformation, whether that word spoken appears to meet the grand standing of intellectualism, or not– it matters nothing. A word from God is one with the Spirit's intent, and indivisible, for God's Word itself is spiritual and breathes truth. A worthy prayer, is

Lord I receive your word from heaven, cleanse me by your Spirit, heal me by your Spirit, strengthen me by your word-my meat, and were word has been spoken in contravention to your word let it cease. May your word proceed as from an undefiled altar and let purifying fire come down from heaven, so our praise will be acceptable. A word not aided by the Spirit is never from God. It's a word from God we need for the hour.

Jesus said in Luke 4:18-21

'The Spirit of the Lord is upon me, <u>because he hath anointed me to preach the gospel to the poor</u>; he hath sent me to heal the broken-hearted, <u>to preach deliverance</u> to the captives, and recovering of sight to the blind, to set at liberty them that are bruised, to preach the acceptable year of the Lord. <u>And he closed the book, and he gave it again to the minister, and sat down</u>. And the eyes of all them that were in the synagogue were fastened on him. <u>And he began to say unto them, This day is this scripture fulfilled in your ears</u>.'

There is power in the word of God. When as a believer of Christ you begin to take time to read, think about and obey God's Word by placing it in your heart it will deliver and transform you. Obedience to God's Word is not torturous, or meant to discourage – rather it's a way of living that we keep you from the enemy's schemes. When our minds sway away, it ought to find its place afresh in the word from and of God. Time over time the word of God teaches us it is better and safer to follow after God. And to know His restoration when in need.

The world that do not know God thinks God's instructions for all is meant to coerce and manipulate belief, as it does [as the world operates in that manner itself with ideas meant to manipulate], how wrong. God has shown us His word as true which produces faith for obedience in us– and then through test of time, we see it is good to trust in God. All by His eternal mercy. Praise God. May God help us continually put our hope and heart in Him.

'... *the word of the Lord endureth for ever. And this is the word which by the gospel is preached unto you.*' 1 Peter 1:25 (1 John 5:3)

XXII

DIVINE LIFE AND ACCEPTABLE FRUIT

Matthew 25:31-46

'When the Son of Man comes in His glory, and all the holy angels with Him, then He will sit on the throne of His glory. All the nations will be gathered before Him, and He will separate them one from another, as a shepherd divides his sheep from the goats. And He will set the sheep on His right hand, but the goats on the left. Then the King will say to those on His right hand, 'Come, you blessed of My Father, inherit the kingdom prepared for you from the foundation of the world: for I was hungry and you gave Me food; I was thirsty and you gave Me drink; I was a stranger and you took Me in; I was naked and you clothed Me; I was sick and you visited Me; I was in prison and you came to Me.'

'Then the righteous will answer Him, saying, 'Lord, when did we see You hungry and feed You, or thirsty and give You drink? When did we see You a stranger and take You in, or naked and clothe You? Or when did we see You sick, or in prison, and come to You?' And the King will answer and say to them, 'Assuredly, I say to you, inasmuch as you did it to one of the least of these My brethren, you did it to Me.'

'Then He will also say to those on the left hand, 'Depart from Me, you cursed, into the everlasting fire prepared for the devil and his angels: for I was hungry and you gave Me no food; I was thirsty and you gave Me no drink; I was a stranger and you did not take Me in, naked and you did not clothe Me, sick and in prison and you did not visit Me.'

'Then they also will answer Him, saying, 'Lord, when did we see You hungry or thirsty or a stranger or naked or sick or in prison, and did not minister to You?' Then He will answer them, saying, 'Assuredly, I say to you, inasmuch as you did not do it to one of the least of these, you did not do it to Me.' And these will go away into everlasting punishment, but the righteous into eternal life.'

Notes from this scriptural context:

i. You are justified by faith in Christ not deeds, albeit a faith producing fruit of righteousness.

ii. It's by connecting with Christ in obedience you receive strength to be spiritually productive.

John 15:4

'Abide in Me, and I in you. As the branch cannot bear fruit of itself unless it abides in the vine, so neither can you unless you abide in Me.'

iii. The manner of our relation with others, irrespective of their state, is often testament of our relationship with Christ. For a renewed heart is inclined to good works.

iv. The great reward awaits the believer when Christ comes in glory, sited on His throne, for work done from the place of faith. It is better in all of our labours not to lose sight of this, as nothing will compare. Faith is not the absence of works, but works is not the basis or foundation, God is, however works is evidence of authentic, sound, genuine faith. Faith is accompanied by works done in righteousness.

Revelation 22:12

'And behold, I am coming quickly, and My reward is with Me, to give to every one according to his work.'

v. Good fruit is from good seed. Christ in you will produce a worthy harvest. This is why the focus is never how can I act differently, but rather how can I come in relationship with Christ. Only God can govern a pure thought and a rightly motivated action.

Luke 6:44

'For every tree is known by its own fruit. For men do not gather figs from thorns, nor do they gather grapes from a bramble bush.'

vi. Jesus Christ reminds us, whatever worthy thing you do to the 'least of these my brethren' you have done to Him. As we prioritise the kingdom and walk in faith, do not forget to show kindness to all like the Samaritan in the scriptures.

Galatians 6:10

'Therefore, as we have opportunity, let us do good to all, especially to those who are of the household of faith.'

vii. Our faith in Christ grants us the opportunity and grace to display the glory of God. For through the death and resurrection of the Lord this is possible, as a seed decays but births a new life. We were created for good works.

Ephesians 2:10.

'For we are His workmanship, created in Christ Jesus for good works, which God prepared beforehand that we should walk in them.'

XXIII

A SOTERIOLOGICAL SHIFT (UNDERSTANDING OF SALVATION) WITH CHRIST AT THE CENTRE

As initially referred to, the Pentecostal (Evangelical and Charismatic) theology at the crux makes *primos* Christology, embedding a narrative of the person of Christ– revolving at the heart of the message. And rightly so, and so should any person that proclaims the gospel prioritise in their message. There is so much an institutional agenda, but there is the need to tell the whole truth of Christ's birth, work on earth, suffering, death, triumphant resurrection and plan for His believers and the nations– where Christ is at work to reconcile human relationship with the Godhead, to impart His kind of life, righteousness and divine nature, to restore man's lost inheritance and authority, and then empowering the believer by baptism of the Spirit in fulfilment of prophecy for Christian service of a supernatural and practical nature and for a godly witness to the nations, for the purpose of others turning to the saving knowledge of the Son (His person) through the preaching of the word of faith. Also, to consider the significance of Christ shapes our eschatological expectation and hope of eternity, where total salvation will be accounted for by Him for complete perfection, in body, soul, and spirit. At the base, the running thread is the power of God as revealed in Christ being able to bring about salvation in its entirety through the work of the Spirit.

The salvation experience is considered one of the most important teachings in Pentecostal and Charismatic movement, and forms the basis of significant study in Christian theology. Early Evangelical tradition and theologians of this worldview share this ideal, to a significant point, as illustrated in the 'fourfold' or 'fivefold' gospel, which some rather describe as the 'full gospel' motif, enumerated as Jesus Christ as Saviour, healer, baptiser of the Holy Spirit, and soon coming King.[8] The fifth further points Christ as the Sanctifier. Archer in his article highlights the work of Donald Dayton as one of the most influential in the emergence of Pentecostal theology. Dayton also agrees with early Pentecostals on the appropriateness of the full gospel in its breadth and preventing reductionism,[9] as necessary, to broaden its tentacles and maintain a vital Christocentric essence without compromising its pneumatology. The Evangelical, Charismatic and Pentecostal soteriological perspective, seem to agree on the Lord Jesus Christ as saviour of mankind, to the one who believes in Him for forgiveness of sins and impartation of the life of God. Some few shaky skirmishes begin to appear as one consult perspectives further, as theologians decipher on the manner of operation of the Spirit or exploration of questions on sanctification. I suggest an approach that invokes a type of systematic theological construct that pinpoints the core and recurrent Pentecostal theme amongst the disparities which is its' Christocentric essence, affirming a trinitarian harmony, of Christ operating by the Spirit in and for God's glory for the purpose of salvation, enabling the Saints to partner in witness and service; also with due diligence to hermeneutical attestations, and in the Church– a living demonstration of the work of the Spirit confirming the word. To recluse the idea of salvation from Pentecostal theology is to frustrate its fibre. Pentecostal theology first, affirms Christ, then His work by the Spirit in and through the believer. The purpose being to save him or her, and then raise an instrument to minister his grace to the world God loves, and that He died for.

A proper construct, true to the early Church father's teachings would identify amongst others core themes, that the scriptures attest to the purpose of Christ to redeem the nations, the need for the preaching of the word of faith and for those who hear to believe and repose trust, faith in Christ, as a matter of genuine change of heart and confession in speech. And as evidence, to possess an overflowing thankfulness for the grace of God, rejoicing in hope and willingness to grow in the things of God. And then the understanding of a spiritual shift, from darkness to light, a passing from death to life, from the Kingdom of satan to the Kingdom of God's dear Son, as once lost but found, as those who were not His people but those now His, chosen, saints, beloved, accepted, those who partake in His nature, a new man, sons of God, sanctified, righteous, as those with the newness of life. This divine reception is occasioned entirely by the grace of Christ and not human works, imputing the mercy of God to those who believe in him, as a gift.

Dale Coutler draws a connection by suggesting a model that grounds on the 'acquisition of God's life and deliverance,' which he illustrates is demonstrated in the ministry of Joseph Hillary King of Pentecostal Holiness Church in the 1930s, and John Lakes' (1870-1935) in South Africa and North America[10]– a sense of the gospel epitomising an inward and practical relevancy to humans. The challenges however existed in the disparity of thoughts as shown in Steven Studebaker's work– highlighting that the bifurcation of Christianity and pneumatology creates an objective and subjective paradigm, where the work of the Spirit is interpreted as merely aiding Christ's work, instead of a consideration of its work in partnership or a conjunctive, where Christ acts in the power of the Spirit.[11] He argues it is Protestant soteriology that has crept into the Pentecostal discourse, subtly and gained scholarly deliberations, as Pentecostal theology should retain the Pneumatological element being very crucial. The partnership of the Spirit then must be reflected as an equally vital constituent with the Trinitarian perspective. I would say that seeing the work of the Spirit either in aid and help of Christ or as an active partner reflecting the synergy of the Godhead in sovereignty but also mutual submission, for the purpose of bringing about salvation as referencing an inner and outward transformative testimony consistent with the teachings of Christ, do not necessarily create a conflicting Pentecostal soteriology. This complementary aspect and multidimensional transformation can be highlighted as a vital element of the Evangelical Pentecostal and Charismatic theology.

Some direct reference to scriptures, I consider key, which I urge you to consider–

From several scriptures the basis for soteriology in Pentecostal [as well as in Charismatic and Evangelical] theology can be gleaned. On the matter of salvation (soteriology), the scriptures should be core. Different traditions within Christianity may differ on styles of worship, perhaps influenced by culture and accepted rules, but on the Lordship of Christ there must be agreement, if such professes to know Him, as a baseline until we all grow into a mature understanding of the things of the Spirit. For your specific considerations on faith through Christ:

i. In 2 Timothy 3:16 the divinity of Christ is revealed as God made manifest in the flesh (bodily form) for the salvation of those who believe[d] including non-jews. As in Romans 10:13 that '*whoever* calls on the name of the Lord shall be saved.'

ii. The salvation experience is similar to that demonstrated in the old testament by Noah, who in *obedience* to God's word prepared an ark for the salvation of his household, all who believed, becoming a 'heir to the righteousness which is according to faith' (Hebrew 11:7; Acts 16:31, Acts 11:13-15; Revelation 3:20)

iii.   Christ during His earthly ministry emphasised the relevance of salvation, admonishing His disciples to rejoice that their names are written in heaven and that He has revealed himself to them, not merely because evil spirits are subject. Luke 10:20- 22; Revelation 20:11-15, 2 Corinthians 1:20-22, Mark 8:37, John 3:16-17, Luke 15:7

iv.   Jesus Christ in His teaching was clear that salvation was found *only* in Him, the God ordained pathway. John 14:6; Matthew 7:13-14; Hebrews 2:3-4. We are justified by faith and have peace with God *through* Jesus Christ our Lord. Romans 5:1-2,5; John 20:24-30; Hebrews 11:6

v.   Christ calls all to seek after Him. Matthew 6:33; John 7:37-38; Jeremiah 33:3; Isaiah 45:18-25; Proverbs 9:10

vi.   Those who believe in Christ do so because they have had an encounter with Christ (God's word revealed) and believed, not just on the basis of another's opinion. John 4:39-42; Acts 8:29-35; Isaiah 1:18

vii.   By relying on Jesus Christ a person is righteous before God. Romans 5:19; John 3:17-18; Zechariah 4:6

viii.   A relationship with God is possible by faith. John 1:12-13; John 14:8-13

ix.   There is always unlimited love from God but a time limit to his saving grace. As we see in the scriptures that there is no need for faith in death and when before God in judgement, because God requires that our believing is now we are in this physical world. Also to understand, that though God wills salvation, but that He has to give up on a soul because of his or her staunch resistance to the Spirit. Genesis 7:15-16; Matthew 24:37; Hebrews 9:27-28; Romans 1:18-32; Genesis 6:3; Psalm 81:11-12; Isaiah 55:6-7; Luke 16:19-31; John 5:24-30; Romans 8:18-23; John 3:16-21.

x.   When a person comes to the saving knowledge of Christ and truly believe, it will surely be evident in his/her confession. The love of God in our heart definitely must overflow in our speech and conduct in several of life's platforms and manifestations, as He wills. 2 Corinthians 4:13-18; Hebrews 13:15-16; Matthew 12:34-37; I Corinthians 12:3; Romans 10:8-9; 1 John 2:22-23; 1 John 4:1-11; Matthew 10:32-33; Acts 8:4; Romans 5:5.

xi.   That believing the gospel for salvation is not mere emotionalism without a basis in historical facts, or pandering to a friend's opinion, but as a result of genuine belief in the work of Christ, even without haven seen Christ physically but believing His testimony and that of the saints. John 17:3; 1 Peter 3:15; John 4:42; Acts 17:11-12; Matthew 7:21; John 20:25-31; Colossians 2:16-17; Hebrews 9:11-15.

xii. The preaching of the word of faith, and reception by the revelation and power of the Spirit, brings salvation. Matthew 16:17; Psalm 119:130; Romans 10:14-17; Hebrews 4:2-3; Psalm 119:162; John 8:30; 2Corinthians 4:4. God will not despise a contrite heart or cast it away. 1 Timothy 1:15-17; Psalm 51:17; Isaiah 55

xiii. Salvation is a free gift from God, not earned materially or by paying any penance. Ephesians 2:8-9; Matthew 10:5-33; Isaiah 55:1-3; Romans 8:32-34; James 1:5; 1 Corinthians 1:30-31.

xiv. God allows supernatural occurrences to aid believing (even though some are still hard-hearted), but we must believe even if He chooses not to show Himself in the manner we want. John 4:48; Matthew 8:5-13; Hebrews 2:1-4; 1Corinthians 14:24-25; Marks 16:20; John 12:37-41; Matthew 11:20-25.

xv. The preaching of the cross, Jesus Christ's redemptive work, is for the lost. Matthew 18:11-14; 1 Peter 2:4-10; Luke 5:27-32; 1 Corinthians 1:18-31.

xvi. Similitude must not replace the substance of faith; not feigning belief and bringing an 'offering' still. It's not the practicalities as much as it is the sincere openness of heart for God. James 1:7-8; Matthew 15:8-9; Isaiah 29:11-24; Galatians 6:7; Hebrews 11:6.

xvii. Self-justification and confidence from observance of moral laws is not God's righteousness, but rather Christ's justification obtained as a spiritual gift. Luke 18:9-27; Matthew 5:6; Isaiah 64:6-7.

xviii. God's plan is good to redeem all people from all nations. Neither is the faith of one authenticated by the preferred exclusion of another or any group. 2 Peter 3:9; Ephesians 3:5-12; 2:8-22; Acts 11:1-18; Isaiah 11:9-10; 56; Acts 10:34; Romans 2:11-16; 10:13.

Getting the full context right

'For what will it profit a man if he gains the whole world and forfeits his soul? Or what shall a man give in return for his soul?−' [*Christ's words*] Matthew 16:26. Pentecostal theology emphases the supernatural dimensions of the Spirit as manifested in the gifts such as visions, prophecy [etc]; freedom of expression in worship and use of bodily gesticulations as appropriate. An aspect of concern is whether certain human attitudes or patterns should concoct or be representative of soteriology of some sort. To force rigidity, where the body is suppressed apart from speech or in some cases silence, may be a compulsory exercise required by other faiths, or prove of internal transformation or reverence, but would represent a distortion and tantamount to lumping all circles within the Christian movements as similar in practice, devoid of unique personalities of those involved or their traditions, nor discretion of the exercise of the Spirit in its manifestation. The Pentecostals have a tendency to show no forced restraint in passion, celebration or overflow of joyfulness, though this is entirely based on the individual's preference, others are encouraged not to have a sense of being encumbered, but consider just how King David danced before the Lord. These attitudes would not define or be reflective of a soteriological experience or explanation, but of particular practices within or without a movement or faith. I would labour subsequently to review a case study of Pentecostal soteriology by a recent article,[12] using that to emphasis my view of how soteriology gains its voice within the walls of Pentecostal and Charismatic thought. The piece comes in handy to explore how to reconcile this theme. She shares the story of a migrant believer who experiences the saving power of God from demonic affliction, as a classic feature of Pentecostal soteriology. I argue that this classification as Pentecostal soteriology is not whole, seems misplaced and may cause confusion. Reasons will be proffered below. The case in hand raises other valid questions as to whether a Christian cannot be said to be saved, where they have a physical disability, sickness, financial difficulty, or a form of satanic attack? While a further scriptural exegesis in a different direction would explore these themes in depth, as in God bringing help or deliverance so they can fully inherit their purpose or promise in Christ, I would rather say what should be contemplated and more helpful is what constitute soteriology in a Pentecostal context– being salvation of the soul through the preaching of the word of faith and impartation of the life of God, devoid of material or otherwise status. This case brings to mind the story of Tabitha and Apostle Peter in the scriptures who despite their salvation experienced life's hardship, but saw respite through divine intervention and their lives were spared or saved.

Dorcas's story: Acts 9:36-43 New King James Version (NKJV).

'At Joppa there was a certain disciple named Tabitha, which is translated Dorcas. This woman was full of good works and charitable deeds which she did. But it happened in those days that she became sick and died. When they had washed her, they laid *her* in an upper room. And since Lydda was near Joppa, and the disciples had heard that Peter was there, they sent two men to him, imploring *him* not to delay in coming to them. Then Peter arose and went with them. When he had come, they brought *him* to the upper room. And all the widows stood by him weeping, showing the tunics and garments which Dorcas had made while she was with them. But Peter put them all out, and knelt down and prayed. And turning to the body he said, 'Tabitha, arise.' And she opened her eyes, and when she saw Peter she sat up. Then he gave her *his* hand and lifted her up; and when he had called the saints and widows, he presented her alive. And it became known throughout all Joppa, and many believed on the Lord. So it was that he stayed many days in Joppa with Simon, a tanner.'

Apostle Peter's story: Acts 12:1-11 (NKJV)

'Now about that time Herod the king stretched out *his* hand to harass some from the church. Then he killed James the brother of John with the sword. And because he saw that it pleased the Jews, he proceeded further to seize Peter also. Now it was *during* the Days of Unleavened Bread. So when he had arrested him, he put *him* in prison, and delivered *him* to four squads of soldiers to keep him, intending to bring him before the people after Passover. Peter was therefore kept in prison, but constant prayer was offered to God for him by the church. And when Herod was about to bring him out, that night Peter was sleeping, bound with two chains between two soldiers; and the guards before the door were keeping the prison. Now behold, an angel of the Lord stood by *him*, and a light shone in the prison; and he struck Peter on the side and raised him up, saying, 'Arise quickly!' And his chains fell off *his* hands. Then the angel said to him, 'Gird yourself and tie on your sandals'; and so he did. And he said to him, 'Put on your garment and follow me.' So he went out and followed him, and did not know that what was done by the angel was real, but thought he was seeing a vision. When they were past the first and the second guard posts, they came to the iron gate that leads to the city, which opened to them of its own accord; and they went out and went down one street, and immediately the angel departed from him. And when Peter had come to himself, he said, 'Now I know for certain that the Lord has sent His angel, and has delivered me from the hand of Herod and *from* all the expectation of the Jewish people.'

The precise facts in Acts 9 and 12 are reproduced above– of Tabitha and Apostle Peter who both as believers of Christ passed through ordeals that required a supernatural intervention to deliver them from it. Dorcas also known as Tabitha, became sick and died but God used Apostle Peter to raise her up and those who had been refreshed by her hospitality ministry rejoiced. However, in contrast to Peter's story, who later down the line was arrested as breaching the laws of the land in his times, for preaching Christ publicly, witnessed a mighty deliverance where an Angel of the Lord rescued him out of prison, then he realised it was not a vision. These 'salvation' experiences may form aspects of witnessing the power of the risen Lord, but do not define Christ's idea of a 'born again' experience, a spiritual rebirth, as indicated in John 3. Hence Pentecostal soteriology deeply and truly represented would be one that recognises the translated state of the believer. As replete in the holy scriptures one that has become a Citizen of heaven because they belong to the living God, part of the Kingdom of light by faith, operating far above satanic affliction by the instrument of God's power, a person with life from God. Not one trying to gain God's love and acceptance, but accepted and sealed by the Holy Spirit. Recognising that except a person comes into relationship with the Lord Jesus Christ they cannot have this life from God.[13] Not discountenancing on the one hand the continued need to work out or continue in salvation, walking in the newness of life, effectively ministering by the power of the Spirit, and living as those saved by the grace of God and renewing our mind to conform fully to his wisdom, but on the other hand bearing in mind that our present body whether dead or alive also awaits redemption when it would put on incorruptible body. In a concise sense, it is consistent with Charismatic, Evangelical, and Pentecostal teachings [scriptures and Christian traditions], to agree that our Spirit is saved, born again by wholeheartedly believing in and confessing Christ, that our soul is being transformed or saved and renewed by the word as we walk with Christ, and that the body though subject to deterioration will be saved from corruption as evidenced by Christ's resurrection from the dead. This is the fulcrum of the soteriological vision envisaged in conversation as it relates to Pentecostalism, beyond miraculous signs or financial blessings, which it does not disapprove of nonetheless. As opposed to passiveness or self-focused 21st century individualistic and control obsessed materialistic culture which focuses usually on how much a person can manipulate events to earn for themselves a better life, Pentecostal theology shifts the focus to Christ being centre. A recognition that the 'horse is prepared' but victory in battle comes from the Lord.[14] This case highlights a minute representation of what 'salvation' entails which seems to ring more a liberalistic theological bell than Pentecostal theology, which although considers financial supply as possible from God but not a core factor or deciding rationale or standard for, or, product of salvation. Miroslav Volf emphasises Pentecostal theology as having a tendency to express salvation as distinguished from the liberationist perspective, as its often seen in the concept of *anihilatio mundi* and *ex nihilo*– which is of God working from above in the affairs of the world to bring individual salvation and transform society, but also expect the end of an evil world and a new creation– again distinguished from liberal theories where the individual's response to the gospel is seen in mainly socio-economic terms, as being more crucial.[15] The arguments attempt however to strike the uniqueness in the synergy in thought, where it concerns the materiality of salvation, which requires that at some level there is the meeting the need of a human being, whether of a spiritual nature or physical. The difference appears to be the soul affection. As Volf notes that Martin Luther's didactic in the reformation period construct a soteriological dimension that points a distinction between the inner and outward man, that a man's salvation has nothing to do with the bodily and earthily realm but that no change for the better in that realm can be understood as an aspect of salvation itself. Pentecostals in modern times prioritise the logic of inner transformation as proof of salvation, but however I agree also emphasise the need for care of outward concern and wellbeing, as an outworking of the inner experience not purely amassing economic gains.

Back to the story of the migrant and a member of a Pentecostal-affiliated Church ministry in Johannesburg in South Africa, who recounts that on one of his visits to another Pentecostal Church in the same city, where in a deliverance service he had a vision of a lizard trapped in a bottle and corked, but a voice said, 'it is you in that jar where they have held you captive. But I am going to set you free today.' Then the jar fell and broke in pieces, then the animal came out and stood there. He thought God was saying that He has brought him salvation–'the bigger power of God for his good.'[16] This being a reflection of satanic curse from his distant family of his home of origin, which has led to his untold suffering abroad, deportation from the United States, separation from family and financial meltdown, all this spanning a long period of time. Jeannarat in her perspective, in the article do not say if this experience is similar to every known patterns in comparison to migrant-controlled [missionary churches] or established churches. However the reductionism and compartmentalisation approach in analysing Chiedu's story do not present a complete soteriology which underlines Pentecostal theology, as it segregates a theological concept on the basis of migration and in the restrictive context of materialistic needs. For instance glossolalia or vibrant expressions in worship, dependence on the Spirit are traits found in variant Pentecostal traditions globally, often with minor emphasis. This do not however holistically explain the varied models present even within Pentecostalism.[17] This situation progresses to him giving his testimony of a turn around after the prayer and revelation, his family is reconciled, a change in political-driven legislation that allows for his resettlement, an improvement in his financial state, though he still expects through faith to tackle what is still left of his challenge. His story is not isolated from the challenge of most persons in the world— black or white, relocating-migrant or indigenes, priviledged or not etc, seeking a greater intervention to help navigate these battles.

As in Dorcas, Apostle Peter, Mr. Chiedu they all experience the saving power of God in their physical predicament and limitation. A soteriology that explains a salvation from these ills but do not focus on the Christological distinctives [what some call the full gospel and the work of the person of the Spirit, as it relates to the context of the whole plan of salvation] will be in the long run ineffective, and misses the real point. So, beyond materialism, wellbeing, it should represent a gospel of soul conversion, the affirmation of the Spirit at work in us, redemption and an eschatological hope; this sound basis, and kind of soteriology prepares a believer to *deal, triumph* and *endure* with delays to a divine promise, manipulations of the wicked person who opposes good, temporary life's challenge, or persecutions to sabotage or supress efforts. Now the believer understands the love of God is beyond things even martyrdom[18] and in seeking first not second, the Kingdom, God is responsible for adding other material needs.[19] Christ is faithful to save the soul and preserve the Spirit of the believer, and even raise the dead– and giving a heavenly body. Fostering this manner of holistic soteriological thought is so central to the Christian belief, of the purpose of Christ. His work is to secure human redemption and reconciliation with the father God for those who believe with the affirmation of the Spirit. Therefore a soteriology void of this principle in any faith or denomination according to the biblical stance, falls flat. I show that soteriology is a very significant thought in Pentecostalism and have similar binding thread with other Christian movements, as least should have at the core. There is almost a trait of Pentecostalism within several denominations in the ecumenical enclave. Essential, however, to contemplate a credible Pentecostal soteriology it must be one with a vibrant Christological focus, justifiable biblically, one that contemplates salvation holistically and transcends a materialistic prerequisite. Basically, to have a credible understanding of faith that is in Christ, you must move away from false media claims, unhelpful representations, and popular cultural ideas that suggest scriptural irrelevance, or conflicting notions on God, as God is not confused to create such. Then begin to engage honestly with the source– the word of God.

PART III BE INSPIRED

Making music in your heart to God– of Him, to Him. These songs and many more that reiterate the awesomeness of God appeal greatly to my heart. God is glorified through those who wrote the lyrics, others who improved on these songs, or compose the music, as well as those who used their God-given influence to spread the songs so many are encouraged. In all, of vital importance is focusing on the words especially when true to scriptures– adoring God, the creator of the heavens and the earth.

XXIV

THREE HYMNS, THREE STORIES AND THEOLOGICAL ANALYSIS– OF ONE GREAT GOD

This part explores three classic hymns, its inherent theological emphasis, and the implications. The selection is 'How Great thou Art,' 'Just as I am without one Plea,' and 'Guide me o thou Great Jehovah.' I write these hymns present themes on the sovereignty, power and greatness of God as seen in creation and ability to alter causes. Also reflected through these hymns, is Christ's redemptive work through his death on the cross and eschatological dimensions. In the context of their unique story, and theology, one can decipher some harmony doctrinally irrespective of varied Christian tradition.

First Hymn

The hymn 'How Great thou Art' extols God for His greatness. The hymn was originally written by Reverend Carl Gustaf Boberg, a Swedish preacher in 1885 when he was 26 years of age, as a poem, but was later found out and made into Swedish folk music.[20] This was later reworked into other languages such as German and Russian prior, but later translated into English by missionaries serving in Poland in about 1933, by Reverend Stuart K. Hine and his wife. Stuart was inspired after the war in that period upon a conscious reflection on the beauty of creation, then added a fourth verse and included it in English hymnal.[21] It has since gained incredible world acclaim, sung in churches, events and homes across the nations in their languages, and unique styles.[22] This song is sacred for many, as it is a timely reminder of God's power so revealed in the intricate and complex design of the universe and our state of dependency. William Clark, of the American University in Bulgaria, in a published research paper[23] quoted Reverend Carl's hymn to buttress the fact that there is an acknowledgement that even within secular and Christian communities that there is a beauty in nature, value systems and sacredness, not so much in itself or one of history but rather one that 'orient the mind and soul of men and women to God as Creator and display His majesty,' and carries with it a responsibility to preserve it. The hymn:

O Lord my God, when I in awesome wonder
Consider all the worlds thy hands have made,
I see the stars, I hear the rolling thunder,
Thy power throughout the universe displayed:

Refrain

Then sings my soul, my Savior God, to thee:
How great thou art! How great thou art!
Then sings my soul, my Savior God, to thee:
How great thou art! How great thou art!

When through the woods and forest glades I wander
And hear the birds sing sweetly in the trees,
When I look down from lofty mountain grandeur,
And hear the brook and feel the gentle breeze:

And when I think that God, his Son not sparing,
Sent him to die, I scarce can take it in,
That on the cross, my burden gladly bearing,
He bled and died to take away my sin.

When Christ shall come with shout of acclamation
And take me home, what joy shall fill my heart!

Then I shall bow in humble adoration,
And there proclaim, My God, how great thou art![24]

Verses one points to God at work in creation, the universe being the work of His hands. The author personalises his visual experience of nature, as one that reminds him of God's power. He writes, 'Thy power throughout the universe displayed.' The refrain further shows the hymn is not only about the greatness of God but also His power to save. Verses Two continues the theme of the beauty of creation by a magnificent and intelligent being. In the third stanza, it has progressed to the theme of salvation which is espoused as available through Christ who died on the cross for sin. In verse four, it is salvation from the earth's decay and fallen nature, to go 'home,' in heaven. An eschatological reflection on the hope of Christ's return. He writes, the very thought fills the heart with joy. The author's song portrays the greatness of God as revealed in nature and the saving work of Christ in redemption from sin and the redemptive hope of his return to take believers to heaven. He personalises this experience in the song, throughout the verses. As we sing we find ourselves joining his testimony as we also realise it is an experience we equally share which makes this song unique. He sings using the pronoun 'I' a lot, saying for instance – as I consider God's work, His power then my heart sings His greatness; that he thinks of His saving work and how He is coming to take him home, 'Then I shall bow in humble adoration, and there proclaim, My God, how great thou art!' In singing the hymn 'How great thou art,' we are forced to decide and concede with this vibrant personal affirmation of the greatness of God.

Second Hymn

The hymn, 'Just as I am without one plea,' hereinafter referred to as 'Just as I am' was written by Charlotte Elliot in 1835, and the music composed by Woodworth Saffron Walden.[25] The story[26] of the song is that a Swiss Evangelist had ministered to Charlotte about her need for a saviour when in London, after sometime of pondering on his teaching, she later asked him how she must go about her conversion. The minister, Cesar Malan, said to her she had nothing of merit to bring to God but she was to come just as she was to Christ and trust Him for salvation. It was on the basis of this she came to faith, and in subsequent years despite her battling fatigue and depression she remembered his words and penned the words in hymn. The song has since ministered to many across the world, and is a notable classic Christian hymn. The 'Just as I am' hymn is reckoned to have had additional notability in Evangelist Billy Graham's meetings usually held across stadiums in America and other nations, because it was almost a permanent feature especially when he made the call for salvation, the song played in the background and was sung by the choir, as he awaits many to make a decision to follow Christ.[27] This is also the case in other congregations, who might sing it during an altar call or afterwards. It's as follows:

Just as I am—without one plea,
But that Thy blood was shed for me,
And that Thou bidst me come to Thee—
O Lamb of God, I come, I come.

Just as I am—and waiting not
To rid my soul of one dark blot,
To Thee whose blood can cleanse each spot—
O Lamb of God, I come, I come.

Just as I am—though tossed about
With many a conflict, many a doubt,
Fightings and fears within, without—
O Lamb of God, I come, I come.

Just as I am—poor, wretched, blind;
Sight, riches, healing of the mind,
Yea, all I need in Thee to find—
O Lamb of God, I come, I come.

Just as I am—Thou wilt receive,
Wilt welcome, pardon, cleanse, relieve;
Because Thy promise I believe—
O Lamb of God, I come, I come.

Just as I am—Thy love unknown
Hath broken every barrier down;
Now, to be Thine, yea, Thine alone—
O Lamb of God, I come, I come.

Just as I am—of that free love
The breadth, length, depth, and height to prove,
Here for a season, then above—
O Lamb of God, I come, I come![28]

The hymn 'Just as I am' emphasises the work of salvation through Christ alone to the believer who responds to God's call to 'come,' take a step towards Christ beckoning by faith. Similarly it adopts a personalised narrative. In verses one, it speaks of a dependency on what God has done through Christ in the shedding of His precious blood. It lays emphasis on justification by faith in Christ in response to God's call. It then in stanza two re-emphasises one comes to Christ just as they are. Without a sense of self-defence but trusting Christ to sanctify by His blood. Verses three and four analysis, shows He says come irrespective of life's difficulty, conflicts, fears, frailties. This is because in the 'Lamb of God,' which is Christ, one can find healing, spiritual sight and true riches. Christ typifies the Lamb of God meant for sacrifice, who takes away the sins of the world. In verse five, Christ promises to 'welcome, pardon, cleanse, relieve' those who believe and come to Him. The hymn in verse six states that barriers of whatever kind are broken by the greatness of His love which is beyond exhaustive knowing. These obstacles that restrains are broken by God's power so that the one who comes might become Christ's. The last stanza also points out the nature of God's love. Not only is He great and unfathomable, to the extent He reveals, He is able to save from sin. He calls the sinner to Himself, and fulfils the promise of salvation to the believer, an offer of love which is free– 'Just as I am—of that free love; the breadth, length, depth, and height to prove; Here for a season, then above—' The hymn also delves into an eschatological theme of the hope of redemption and spending eternity with God. Finally, is the resounding words of 'o Lamb of God, I come, I come!.' Speaking of surrender to the purposes of God in faith. The hymn is filled with the spirit of determination to grasp the call of God. It shows the understanding that this call and redemption is a work of grace as there is no plea to make, neither is it a divine forceful attempt to coerce the human, or worthiness in self. He cries voluntarily, in submission, I come, as I am, but to a great God able to transform and redeem. It is about relinquishing trust in self, knowing God would accept us in the midst of our vulnerabilities, so the one who comes, comes for help and mercy, joyfully and thankfully.

Third Hymn

My third selection, is another classic hymn that has inspired many. It was written by William William (1717- 1791) a Welsh Methodist preacher, and was translated into English by Peter Williams. Reverend Williams Williams was himself encouraged by the ministry of Welsh Evangelist Harris Howell, and decided to be a preacher after being under his ministration. He is recorded to have travelled over 100,000 miles on horseback to preach across Wales and to have written over 800 hymns.[29] It says,

Guide me, O Thou great Jehovah,
[or Guide me, O Thou great Redeemer...]
Pilgrim through this barren land.
I am weak, but Thou art mighty;
Hold me with Thy powerful hand.
Bread of Heaven, Bread of Heaven,
Feed me till I want no more;
Feed me till I want no more.

Open now the crystal fountain,
Whence the healing stream doth flow;
Let the fire and cloudy pillar
Lead me all my journey through.
Strong deliverer, strong deliverer,
Be Thou still my strength and shield;
Be Thou still my strength and shield.

Lord, I trust Thy mighty power,
Wondrous are Thy works of old;

Thou deliver'st Thine from thralldom,
Who for naught themselves had sold:
Thou didst conquer, Thou didst conquer,
Sin, and Satan and the grave,
Sin, and Satan and the grave.

When I tread the verge of Jordan,
Bid my anxious fears subside;
Death of deaths, and hell's destruction,
Land me safe on Canaan's side.
Songs of praises, songs of praises,
I will ever give to Thee;
I will ever give to Thee.

Musing on my habitation,
Musing on my heav'nly home,
Fills my soul with holy longings:
Come, my Jesus, quickly come;
Vanity is all I see;
Lord, I long to be with Thee!
Lord, I long to be with Thee![30]

This hymn focuses on God– His greatness, power to save from sin, from every life's difficulty and the vestiges of a decaying world with a present hope of eternity in perspective. The very first stanza of 'Guide me, o thou great Jehovah,' calls out to a great God. It declares the strength of God and asks Him for leadership and direction. To show God's strength it calls God 'great Jehovah,' 'mighty one,' with a 'powerful hand.' For divine strength there is an awareness for dependency on only the invisible God to hold, and support his weakness in a hard-pressed path, but the author also longs for God to feed him to the full. As strength to the body naturally comes after eating food to the full, there is an analogy of the need to be satisfied with 'bread from heaven–' being spiritual food for nourishing. The second stanza he asks for the stream of water to flow– 'open now the crystal fountain.' Again, to the theme of strength from God, in leadership and direction, the writer asks for help and protection– 'Be thou still my strength and shield.' In verse three the theme of divine strength continues as he reminds God of what He did in times past, of His ability to save from 'thralldom–' a reference in earlier period of the system of subjugation or slavery in fiercest terms. He declares the victory of Christ against 'sin, Satan and the grave.' Into the other stanzas four and five, the hymn writer ponders the end of days on earth and judgement, and prays for God to redeem his soul as he spends eternity in His praise– 'land me safe on Canaan's side.' A reference to a place of promise for God's children who trust him, from bondage to freedom, as in the exodus of the people of Israel from Egypt to a prosperous place. In the song there is a looking forward to, but also a deep assurance of being part of that hope, though being here on earth and longing to be with Christ in fulfilment. And the thought of this fills the heart with joy. It is the balance of humility in the prayer and the blessed assurance of a faithful God who keeps His promise to save body, soul and spirit in this life and that to come. The hymn is a prayer for God to lead the believer in this sojourn on earth as one looks on to a future afterwards with God.

Theological emphasis

These three songs are great ways to express faith – 'How great thou art,' 'Just as I am' and 'Guide me, o thou great Jehovah' in many ways reflect similar themes of the greatness of God, the believer's dependency on His greatness to save in every way, whether be of the challenge of living in a body and the external pressures that brings. A reminder of the corruption of the soul without Christ but the joy of the life God's Spirit brings in the believer. All the three hymns even seem to have the same progression in thought as well, though not the same stanzas. It however does not come as a surprise the similarity in thought. The anticipation of the life afterwards would be the last emphasis in the verses, as this would be the normal course of events if Christ tarries. Eschatology contemplates the end of all things, Christ's return, His judgements and the saints' reign with Christ. Theologically the hymns lay recurring emphasis of

God's sovereignty in creation and power, also a soteriological perspective on Christ saving work through His atoning sacrifice for sin, as well as eschatological emphasis of hope and joy to be found in being with Christ. None of the hymn suggest an end to all that is life here on earth, they ring the anticipation of a glorious after-life, powerful enough to sooth any present ill. I think these hymns find broad consensus scripturally on principles of faith in Christ alone for redemption and forgiveness of sins, through his death and resurrection; and amongst different Christian traditions— Evangelical, Charismatic, and Pentecostal denominations, and perhaps other groups. This affirmation is in the sense that in the songs, the doctrine of trinity, the Godhead nature of God the Father, God the Son, and God the Holy Spirit as equal in sovereignty, power and eternal, is not compromised. Also in these traditions they share certain core doctrinal 'distinctives,' in four parts, that marks commonality in the teaching, some of which are reflected in the hymns and not contradicted.[31] That is, recognising Christ as Saviour, Christ as healer, Christ as the baptiser of the Spirit and Jesus Christ as the soon coming King. Some contemplate a fifth, which is Christ as sanctifier.[32] As from the lyrics, the Christocentric emphasis as distinctively categorised is reflected, which means there is really no theological or doctrinal issue raise, this would explain why these hymns are very popular amongst these faith traditions. The theological basis of these hymns would be authentic where they have a foundational basis in the biblical scriptures. When sung, there is an encouragement to be reflective on the words, as they are also a basis for teaching young converts principles on Christ and His work, and the hope that awaits. The tone and style of music sometimes reflect this.

On the Sovereignty of God in creation, and His ability to give victory over troubles, Isaiah 45:5-7 is a sound reference point, for the hymns, It says, '*I am the Lord, and there is no other; There is no God besides Me. I will gird you, though you have not known Me, that they may know from the rising of the sun to its setting that there is none besides Me. I am the Lord, and there is no other; I form the light and create darkness, I make peace and create calamity; I, the Lord, do all these things.*' This is about a God who displays His power in the universe, the one who is able to deal with whatever conflict, fears or doubts; but also in the third hymn is the Great Jehovah. Psalm 46:10, also says, '*Be still, and know that I am God; I will be exalted among the nations, I will be exalted in the earth!*' There is a theological basis, when in context of God's power, creative ability, and sovereignty. Another applicable verse is Psalm 19 [TLB] it says, '*The heavens are telling the glory of God; they are a marvellous display of his craftsmanship. Day and night they keep on telling about God. Without a sound or word, silent in the skies, their message reaches out to all the world. The sun lives in the heavens where God placed it and moves out across the skies as radiant as a bridegroom going to his wedding, or as joyous as an athlete looking forward to a race! The sun crosses the heavens from end to end, and nothing can hide from its heat. God's laws are perfect. They protect us, make us wise, and give us joy and light.'*

Furthermore, with regard to the theme of God's redemptive plan and ability as replete in the hymns, in the scriptures we find Romans 10:12-13, which says 'For there is no distinction between Jew and Greek, for the same Lord over all is rich to all who call upon Him. For 'whoever calls on the name of the Lord shall be saved.' Also in Romans 8, it says, 'There *is* therefore now no condemnation to those who are in Christ Jesus, who do not walk according to the flesh, but according to the Spirit. For the law of the Spirit of life in Christ Jesus has made me free from the law of sin and death.' This is similarly in the more popular verses of John 3:16-17, which all highlight that Christ frees the one who comes to Him or calls on Him, believing for salvation, responding in faith. God gave His Son for the redemption of the world, and Christ paid the price in full.

In addition to the theme of God's sovereign power, His redemption, is the theological ambit of Christ's return also touched in these hymns. Also scripturally astute, as we see in John 14 (NIV), the Lord Himself saying, '*Do not let your hearts be troubled. You believe in God; believe also in me. My Father's house has many rooms; if that were not so, would I have told you that I am going there to prepare a place for you? And if I go and prepare a place for you, I will come back and take you to be with me that you also may be where I am. You know the way to the place where I am going.*' Here makes a promise of a home above, and are already part of that family by faith in Jesus, we only change location on demise to unite with God. 1Thessalonian 4 13-18, assures the believer of Christ– Apostle Paul's writing, '*But I do not want you to be ignorant, brethren, concerning those who have fallen asleep, lest you sorrow as others who have no hope. For if we believe that Jesus died and rose again, even so God will bring with Him those who sleep in Jesus. For this we say to you by the word of the Lord, that we who are alive and remain until the coming of the Lord will by no means precede those who are asleep. For the Lord Himself will descend from heaven with a shout, with the voice of an archangel, and with the trumpet of God. And the dead in Christ will rise first. Then we who are alive and remain shall be caught up together with them in the clouds to meet the Lord in the air. And thus we shall always be with the Lord. Therefore comfort one another with these words.*' From the writing to the Thessalonians, we see Paul rehashing the Lord's promise (also found in Acts 1:6-11), but we can also appreciate the comfort in the hymns– as in Rev. Stuart's fourth stanza addition in 'How Great though Art' where he says of the joy that will fill his heart when God comes take him home, as he bows in humble adoration, and also in the earnest beckoning of the Lord to come 'quickly' in Rev. William's plea in the last stanza of 'Guide me o thou Great Jehovah.' Similarly, as Rev Cesar's teaching comes to mind in Charlotte Elliot's penned words– 'Here for a season, then above.' There is something always, and unfadingly reassuring to meet Christ face to face, and to rest from all our Christian labours, when all the purpose for which we were called specifically to glorify Christ in this earth is finished and the important work of reaching out to save the lost is done. In conclusion, what an assurance to have, that this fleeting and often turbulent life do not represent all the believer of Christ hopes for. Drawing inspiration from the hymns, to take cognisance and give thanks for the glory of God revealed in nature, and His work in redemption from sin, with rejoicing having an expectation of Christ's return, and if He tarries to be with Him in eternity.

Some lyrics– Spirit inspired:

This is what matters to me my dearest, God

To see your glory
To seat at your feet
And daily feed on your revelation
To raise an alarm of praise with a thankful heart.

What can be better?
What can be greater?
To worship God, and behold His face
And to rejoice in His salvation and deliverances
This is what matters truly to be my dearest, God.

To ponder on His truth
And leap for joy at the blessing of each understanding
To honour Him still
And to see how enriching and endless His testimonies are.

These things you hide from the shamelessly proud
And reveal to the humble at heart
Now the openhearted is filled
To enjoy the delicacy of knowing the mystery of heaven.

Now after receiving your blessed Holy Spirit
Because I gave you my heart by faith,
By grace I understand why I must spend eternity in endless praise– having your seal,

Will be a priviledge and a joy— as it doesn't weary
me now in His presence, it wouldn't then.[33]

The sovereign and great God

After seeing your gracious nails pierced hands by
faith
And the effects of your bruised side
To heal a skewed conscience and set my inheritance
in heaven
Now I receive insight to worship you
Jesus Christ, Son of the Living God

I worship you the only true Lord
Lord of heaven and earth, father God
Lord of all, Lord alone
Lord above gods of the earth

The intricate design of the flower speaks
The precision and beauty, yes, speaks volumes
The earth hung in space declares greatness
Even the small-scale of human manufacturing can't
match your greatness

Minds change with time, and theories amend
But your great name won't
The honour of your name makes your words
fearsome

Your present miraculous interventions, and our
limitation to controlling nature
Surely avert our minds to you

It is better to have you fight my battles
You do a thorough job and I'm blame-free
Spirits don't get sued in human law courts
They don't fret or pander for favours– they are
God's subjects
They do His bidding and execute His justice
I allow Him instruct them for my good– it is far
better and peaceable[34]

XXV

THIS SAME JESUS CHRIST, WILL RETURN IN SAME MANNER YOU SAW HIM TAKEN UP

Acts 1:4-12, shows us the last hours narrative of the life of Jesus Christ here on earth, and His promise to return.

'And being assembled together with them, He commanded them not to depart from Jerusalem, but to wait for the Promise of the Father, 'which,' He said, 'you have heard from Me; for John truly baptised with water, but you shall be baptised with the Holy Spirit not many days from now.' Therefore, when they had come together, they asked Him, saying, 'Lord, will You at this time restore the kingdom to Israel?' And He said to them, 'It

is not for you to know the times and seasons which the Father has put in His own authority. But you shall receive power when the Holy Spirit has come upon you; and you shall be witnesses to Me in Jerusalem, and in all Judea and Samaria, and to the end of the earth.' Now when He had spoken these things, while they watched, He was taken up, and a cloud received Him out of their sight. And while they looked steadfastly toward heaven as He went up, behold, two men stood by them in white apparel, who also said, 'Men of Galilee, why do you stand gazing up into heaven? This same Jesus, who was taken up from you into heaven, will so come in like manner as you saw Him go into heaven.' Then they returned to Jerusalem from the mount called Olivet, which is near Jerusalem, a Sabbath day's journey.'

John 14:1-6, the words of Jesus Christ to his disciples–

'Let not your heart be troubled; you believe in God, believe also in Me. In my Father's house are many mansions; if it were not so, I would have told you. I go to prepare a place you. And if I go and prepare a place for you, I will come again and receive you to Myself; that where I am, there you may be also. And where I go you know, and the way you know. Thomas said to Him, 'Lord, we do not know where You are going, and how can we know the way?' Jesus said to him, 'I am the way, the truth, and the life. No one comes to the Father except through Me.'

Consider Christ's analogy of what the time spoken of will look like– Matthew 24:36-44,

'But of that day and hour no one knows, not even the angels of heaven, but my Father only. But as the days of Noah were, so also will the coming of the Son of Man be. For as in the days before the flood, they were eating and drinking, marrying and giving in marriage, until the day that Noah entered the ark, and did not know until the flood came and took them all away, so also will the coming of the Son of Man be. Then two men will be in the field: one will be taken and the other left. Two women will be grinding the mill: one will be taken and the other left. Watch therefore, for you do not know what hour your Lord is coming. But know this, that if the master of the house had known what hour the thief would come, he would have watched and not allowed his house to be broken into. Therefore you also be ready, for the Son of Man is coming at an hour you do not expect.'

I think these are *three* pillar-scriptures that enunciate clearly the promise of the Lord's return– with God's sovereign discretion as to the precise exactitude of the time and manner of this occurrence. This challenges us in relation to the matter of preparedness and also fills us with hope as one looks forward to the dawning of perfection for all things. I now subsequently consider some of the discussions over the centuries, which has arisen concerning this, and how Pentecostal, Charismatic and Evangelical Christian traditions have enriched this conversation. As one focuses on the core of the certainty of His return, as admitted by any true believer and assented by scripture, you draw hope and comfort from that, and actually you allow the joy of the Lord to fill your soul, and not be lost in the intensity filled arguments of the structure of happenings especially where without scriptural proof but speculations. The awareness of previous mistakes of forced dates and erroneous prophecies, and unhelpful submissions hopefully will help us exact more caution as we reject what is unhelpful. This is so your Spirit can be open like Apostle John, to pray, 'even so, come Lord Jesus.' Not a sense of hurried escapism but a reluctance to compare anything with seeing Christ, or hold steadfastly to anything but Christ, not one inch of time before He is ready to receive me or one inch of time late. In your time, even so, come Lord Jesus.

Theological notions on eschatology and its relation to Pentecostalism

The complexity of arguments that envelops eschatology is bewildering and deep, as it contemplates boldly the imminent future, thousands of years to come, and how all that relates to the now, of course from a biblical stand point.

There seems to be a correlation between the eschatological viewpoint a Christian hold and their denominational affiliation, not necessarily in all cases. Peter Hocken, reckons eschatology as a 'science of ultimate destiny' which 'shapes' our Christian life and provides the 'contours for our understanding of the present and past.'[35] This nonetheless should restrain us from making up premonitions, but drawing from biblical resource to interpret the future. There is however a recognition that over the centuries interpretations have varied, and there exist key differences between the Evangelical-Pentecostal and Orthodox-Catholic standpoints but also 'complementarity of the fundamental convictions.'[36] And even within denominations itself. Beyond the certainty of Christ's return, is questions of the role of the Church pre and post *Parousia*, the influence of historicity, how academic theological scholars also play a role to shape this debate, and on whether ecumenism is an essential part of the preceding factor, and harmonising biblical interpretations. Pentecostal eschatology, however, has its' distinctive characteristics. The complex nature is almost recognisable by most biblical scholars.[37]

Glenn Balfour writes that Pentecostalism has morphed from solely being identifiable by its pneumatology to a consideration of its eschatological position that also makes it distinct from other faith groups.[38] Given there are varied Pentecostal classifications, more prominent is the Classical Pentecostalism which is more recognised world-wide,[39] as it teaches a reliance on the work of the Holy Spirit and the manifestation of the gifts of the Spirit in the Church today, such as speaking in tongues– *glossolalia,* as well as its evangelisation and doctrinally being Christ-focused as expressed in the full gospel motif. Recently though, Pentecostalism tend to more generally mean Classical Pentecostalism. But for articulating thoughts on eschatology, Balfour thinks in the strict sense there is no such thing as 'Pentecostal eschatology,' as there is not one position but sets of views within Pentecostalism. For instance, where some 20th century Pentecostals would have had some dispensationalist views as oriented from John Nelson Darby's, known for their cessationist position on the gift of tongues,[40] early classical Pentecostals maintain a different position, not just the belief in the Spirit's work of regeneration but a manifestation of all the gifts of the Spirit. Balfour argues for the description 'Pentecostal eschatological distinctives' to be used.[41] Theologians, in some cases tend to construe Pentecostal eschatology as classical Pentecostalism, but agreed they bear the distinctives as highlighted by Balfour– they are three, which are the notion of Premillennialism, emphasis on the significance of nation of Israel, and imminent futuristic eschatology.[42] Calvin Smith criticises the premillennialism as being 'pessimistic' as it envisages an apocalyptic end-time scenario.[43] If this is scriptural portrayal of the end time, reinventing more soothing scenarios and interpretation is one Christians have to be wary about, as that would be an indication the signs of the times, where people will hardly endure gospel truths, as cautioned in Apostle Paul's teachings.[44] 'Imminent futuristic eschatology' however contemplates with a 'strong conviction' that Jesus Christ will return very soon[45]– some have made the mistake of putting dates to it, anticipating it in their lifetime. Premillennialism goes a step further that not only will the Lord return, He will reign on the earth for a 1,000 year period– there are other components to this supposition, as the rapture of the saints, the preceding seven year tribulation period, the return of Christ to defeat His enemies at the battle of Armageddon and rescue the saints and Israel, and casting Satan into the pit and the reign of Christ for 1,000 years, the release of Satan after this duration for a brief time before the battle of Gog and Magog, then the end of all things[46]– the judgement of both the small and great. Also is the category, on the prophetic implications of the nation of Israel. The restoration of the nation of Israel in 1948, and her developments point to theological persuasions such as arguments on Replacement theology,[47] the fulfilment of bible prophecies in the regathering of the Jews from different nations, the people of God according to the promise to Abraham, and Gentile nations grafted into the promise through faith in Christ– how this shapes our respective eschatological hope.[48] As God has not cast us off His people but provided a sacrifice for all.

Furthermore, dispensationalism also has an influence in Pentecostal eschatology, though not without some confusions,[49] however its proposition is a consideration that Israel and the Church has distinct characterisation, and unique plans in God's agenda, also that whilst the Church looks forward to the rapture, Israel comes after; and then the Church age.[50] The complexity perhaps exists in the fact that whilst all premillennialist are dispensationalist, not all dispensationalist hold the pre-tribulation view, and also on the Church- Israel relationship, if it replaces it fully.[51] Some theologians would prefer to consider Pentecostal theology as dispensational premillennialism, others as premillennialism. For instance, its' been noted classical Pentecostalism in Nicaragua identifies as premillennialist in the 1980s.[52] Peter Althouse considers Pentecostal and Charismatic eschatological opinions have been more influenced by dispensational premillennialism, as it emphasises our being in a time where we expect and witness the outpouring of the Spirit prior to the coming of the Lord.[53] Althouse, also expresses the idea that in developing our understanding of eschatology it has to go beyond the redemption of the soul only, to God transforming the entire universe, both its social and cosmic dimensions.[54] Those who ascribe to the millennialist view hold that God's judgement will come on the world and he will transform it and establish His divine reign for a thousand years, though this is not the only variant as mentioned.[55] Also, noteworthy is the efforts of Tim LaHaye, Left Behind series, amongst other authors and academicians, which has made Pentecostal eschatology very popular.[56]

The common biblical references to justify these positions is found in 1 Thessalonians 4:13-18 (Revelations 20, Matthew 24)

But I do not want you to be ignorant, brethren, concerning those who have fallen asleep, lest you sorrow as others who have no hope. For if we believe that Jesus died and rose again, even so God will bring with Him those who sleep in Jesus. For this we say to you by the word of the Lord, that we who are alive and remain until the coming of the Lord will by no means precede those who are asleep. For the Lord Himself will descend from heaven with a shout, with the voice of an archangel, and with the trumpet of God. And the dead in Christ will rise first. Then we who are alive and remain shall be caught up together with them in the clouds to meet the

Lord in the air. And thus we shall always be with the Lord. Therefore comfort one another with these words.'

Historical challenges spanning centuries, facing disillusionment and progressing understanding

As to when this millennium starts, there has been some substantial disagreements, and often times failed predictions. Those who made specific predictions as to when the Lord would come and His reign begin often died without seeing it happen in their days as they insisted must, or if they lived, watched the date announced roll by. In the 2nd century Priscilla and Maximila had both being reckoned to have said the world's demise would be in their days but this didn't happen, as she died in 179CE.[57] In fact Althouse writes that– 'Prophets of millennial expectation and predictions of the imminent end arose occasionally throughout the next four hundred years. Prediction became the fodder of millennialism as charismatic Prophets interpreted biblical prophecy according to current historical events and offered predictions as to the exact time for Christ's return.'[58] The error of such predictions is the overlooking of Christ's words that it has not been given to us to know the exact time set for His return, but to know the signs of the time.[59] Notwithstanding there is the growing understanding that the Prophetic ministry is to affirm the word not create or conjure apostate doctrines.[60] Though He gives us the signs to show us that we are in the times spoken of, not the detail of the date, hour, or minutes. This is a preferred burden not to bear. In the period of Lutheran reformation, an Anabaptist, by name Melchior Hoffman had proclaimed the Lord's return will be in 1533 in Strasbourg, also Johann Albrecht Bengal, a Pietist, predicted it will be in 1836, but neither saw it in the respective dates; this was followed by the complex theological calculations and analysis developed by William Miller, a Baptist, but later became founder of the Seventh-day Adventist Church in the 19th century, who had hoped for the return to be sometime in 1843, and later he revised the date to 1844– none came to be millennial commencement dates.[61] These dates do not disapprove the Lord's return or its authenticity as enunciated in scriptures, nor do the dates compel forcefully His return as we see, but it rather forces us to turn again to the scriptures as we examine carefully what it really said. Also in the 19th century, it is recalled that Charles Taze Russell who founded Watchtower Bible and Tract Society, which became Jehovah's Witnesses, irrespective of the numerous failed precedents, also declared that millennialism had culminated in 1874 and the Lord would come about forty years later, so by 1914 nonetheless it was the same scenario as some of the predictors before him.[62] Althouse writes— 'the disillusionment that comes to expectant Christians when the return of Christ does not occur as predicted, has placed millennialism in a minority position in the broad contours of Christian eschatology.'[63]

Anton Houtepen argues that there is a sense that some theologians conceptualise the end of age, or eschatology, in a 'non-interventionist' basis, of God's relationship with the world— the argument proffered as explanation to modern atheistic thinking that 'the secrets of life and the mysteries of the cosmos are no longer revealed through the 'apocalypses' of visionaries and dreamers, but through sober scientific exploration of the laws of nature, which is core-business of the process of modernisation and rationalisation all over the world.'[64] Notwithstanding, a return to core biblical foundations is the path to stemming a tide of disillusionment, rather than taking God out of the picture and relying on perceived practicalities or man-made systems in itself.

Conceivably, there is need to distinguish individual interpretations or false prophecies, and the written word— which may be disagreed with, but through the centuries has stayed constant. This disillusionment in my view will disperse if you consider that since the 2nd century— 2000 years later, there appear to be stronger evidence for the word than against. Althouse, however highlights that this 'problem of millennial disconfirmation' is solved by ascribing to the view that 'prophecy calculations of the old covenant did not apply to the age of the Church, because God was acting in grace to redeem the Church.'[65] The challenge for the Pentecostal and Charismatic Church would be the extent its eschatological theology would play a significant role and influence the thinking in a secularised society, as Anton Houtepen argues that there is a 'crisis in eschatological thinking' and the need to ponder how not to repeat some of the misconceptions of the 20th century in the 21st century, but figure out ways to 'lay down some possible stepping stones' in terms of the eschatological interpretation theologians favour.'[66] The ecumenical Church appears to have got the fundamental foundational doctrine on salvation, as anchored on Christ's sacrifice, it has to wrestle to find a perfectly unified position on her eschatology. There appears however to be some consensus that the Lord is definitely to return, but with a disparity as to the time and manner. I would refer you to the scriptures, 1 Thessalonians 4, and the three other scriptures cited earlier, to hold the Lord promises to return, and as to the time no one knows; and also that His return would be a public declaration of triumph. This we can begin to build on.

Pentecostal and Charismatic eschatology theology as tool for social activism, articulating sound biblical truth, and managing tensions

The role Pentecostal eschatology leads appear to be one of helping to shape the believer's understanding of what is to come and how to live an authentic Christian life that we have received by faith now. Also, on how to manage the tensions and challenges of waiting, whist exercising Christian living. And that also a proper eschatology operates to preserve sound doctrine. There is the question of whether we should embrace forced ecumenism at all cost, and what influence that brings?

On motivating social engagement

When Murray Dempster weighs in on defusing the anxiety and misconception of eschatological implications– he argues in a slightly different sense, that even in Pentecostal circles the return of Christ is used often as a way of avoiding arguments, especially when the Church is supposed to be of earthly relevance and effecting social change[67]– 'because the second coming of Christ is interpreted as an imminent, apocalyptic event that will trigger the annihilation of the world, social service and social action are typically cast as meaningless human work in an ultimate sense.'[68] Nor is this desperation helped where the Church's social concern is seen as a means to hasten Christ's return. Dempster argues for a 'radical shift in consciousness,' this is where Christ's own framework and conception of the Kingdom is utilised, which is what he calls an 'already-not yet' character.[69] Similar to some other modern Pentecostal theologians, who may choose to express the syllables apart, an 'already' and 'not yet' axis of explaining the revelation of the coming of the Kingdom of Christ. He holds the view that this interpretation would serve as a 'powerful motivation for Christian social concern,' 'a driving force for evangelism.'[70] Reason being, that we then see that the intention of Christ and the import of His ministry, in consideration of His declaration in Luke 4:18-19, was to establish an 'eschatological continuity' between God's reign already and the 'consummated' God's reign to come through Christ.[71] Pentecostal eschatology then operates to shape effective missiology. A practical example of the growing social concern of Pentecostals, is that of the work of Teen Challenge in America, established by David Wilkerson in 1958, he served as an Assemblies of God Pastor, and supported programmes that offered housing and rehabilitation in about several centres across the world with thousands of beds available.[72] And their service has a spiritual component of prayer and ministry to those who came in in need, and they had recordings of testimony of the impact.[73]

It is not necessarily propagating social concern as a means of hastening His return but preaching the gospel so souls will be saved. Where we convey Christ's love, and His teachings because of the love of God in our hearts, for His glory and a yearning to see the lost saved, not just as a matter of mere obligations, then we do well as Christians and advance the testimony of Christ. This is not so much mechanically ticking the box and selfishly anticipating His return, it is more about how we engage spiritually with the Lord now to fulfil His purposes rather than being fixated on the specific time.[74]

Managing Tensions

Essentially, eschatology is about managing the *tension* between the present and the future, which is the 'already' and 'not yet' coming Kingdom of God.[75] The tension is not only that of hope on the one hand and despair on the other, but one of how to navigate understanding the Kingdom within the believer of Christ and that to be revealed– the Kingdom already and that which is to come. The Kingdom of God is established where Christ is, His power and His glory, He is with us as He is in us by His Spirit.[76] Yet we look forward to His literal coming to establishing His Kingdom. Also of living the Christian life in the midst of opposition and the tension that that creates now as we await His return. Althouse suggests 'the eschatological vision of the coming of God can bring great despair in the dread of divine judgement on this world and the creatures that inhabit it, or the eschatological vision can bring great hope in the culmination of divine purposes in the spiritual and material redemption of humanity, the world, and the cosmic orders of the universe.'[77] Also the tension created by the dichotomy of the now and the future– the 'already' of the Kingdom of God, Thompson argues it is indicative of salvation received through the work of Christ, by Christ's justification and the sanctifying work of the Holy Spirit, however, the 'provisional' classification shows we still await 'its final fulfilment in the 'not yet' of the eschaton.'[78] Thompson argues that that the distinctiveness of Pentecostalism motif has an eschatological reach, in essence as believers trust God to experience all fivefold dimensions, of Christ as Saviour, Sanctifier, baptiser of the Holy Spirit, Healer and soon coming King.[79] This also encapsulating the now and future, the un-contradictory nature of it being fulfilled and to be fulfilled, for instance, seeing God as the one who saves and redeems the soul and has given His Spirit, and will save His people in redemption of the body. Thompson argues the fulfilment in healing, is God making all things whole and healed– and then the cosmos and all within it, in its entirety, where the Spirit's work will be perfected in us in power and intimacy; and also in regard of the baptism of the Spirit and speaking in tongues, this will cease in the future but we will be able to 'express accurately intimacy with the Father, Son and Spirit.'[80] Also as we are sanctified by His Spirit then is to experience the regeneration with all creation, in the 'full presence of the trinity in God's holy city, the new Jerusalem,'[81] for Christ who is with us by His Spirit promises to come again soon and reign. The awareness of the implication of waiting for the hope revealed and the presence of Christ with us now eases any tension, as we are comforted and not in dread of judgement as a believer.

The believer's calling presupposes the challenge to live with appropriate eschatological urgency.[82] Julie Ma argues that Christians should focus on the eschatological implications and not be tied up by materialistic and sinful living, but rather take proclaiming of the faith in Christ seriously– not only in word but deeds. Its' a challenge, Ma puts forward this argument especially to Christians 'living in a relativistic, materialistic, and pluralistic society where we can easily lose these fundamental demands of Christian life,' to live with an 'authentic character.'[83]

In Christian mission, the essence is not only the spread of the message of faith and hope, but essentially a 'transformation of life.'[84] Calvin Smith highlights the case of visible example as in Nicaragua in the 1980s, in the Sandinista communist government, where the Church saw fierce opposition for its stand on certain revolutionary policies.[85] They were seen as 'only interested in evangelising the lost.'[86] The tensions was so palpable as it challenged their Christian living and caused much difficulty, in tortures and arrests, to the extent it is claimed 'Nicaraguan Pentecostals genuinely began to wonder if they were living in the last days and if they were experiencing first-hand the birth pangs of the Great Tribulation.'[87]

Dempster, Ma and Smith agree on these tensions, of the already– not yet dynamic, and especially as it relates to living out the Kingdom and looking forward to His return, also as seen in the Church's response to social concerns. There is an encouragement through eschatology, of the hope that a believer can find in trusting Christ. In this present time as the difficulty in the world unravels, to know of the comfort that awaits. Also to expect Christ's solace in the midst of the struggle through His Holy Spirit, the comforter, who enables us to persevere in persecution and trials as we await His coming, rejoicing in hope.[88] Daniel Castelo encourages Christians that 'rather than assuming the modern virtues of individuality and self-reliance, Pentecostals can tarry in courage with the belief that what God has demonstrated to those who love and believe in Him will one day be fulfilled in the Kingdom to come.'[89]

Identifying with biblical truth

Pentecostal eschatology is poised to articulate the truth of the scripture, and allow sound doctrine to flourish, not presumptions, or more optimistic arguments flawed by scripture, but to support contours of hope with scriptural assent. 'Pentecostals share with the Orthodox the view that the Church cannot guarantee the truth by binding the conscience of believers. Only the Spirit can liberate the heart and mind to see the truth evident in the Church's claim.'[90] Julie Ma argues that it seems less a problem of whether Christ spoke of His return more, but 'when–' She succinctly acknowledges this fact– 'The Scriptures abound with statements of Christ's return, and in fact, soon. The prolonged delay of the 'soon' return has understandably created different ways to interpret this to mean something else'[91] Julie argues that Matthew 24:14 which says the 'gospel of the Kingdom will be preached in the whole world as a testimony to all nations; and then the end will come,' operates as a divine sign.[92] The testimony is a witness that all nations have heard of the good news for salvation, and had an opportunity to make a decision. The duty of the believer is to carry on the mandate of Christ, even as He tarries, that the gospel is preached in all corners of the earth. Albeit, the true gospel of hope to all people. It is a sense of resting in the Saviour's love and looking forward to His return, but engaging now in His service and fellowship with believers. 1 Corinthians 11:24 says, 'For every time you eat this bread and drink this cup, you are announcing the Lord's death until he comes again.' The Lord's Supper as a biblical ordinance puts us in remembrance of Christ's sacrifice for us, as we fellowship with other saints in unity. It's a practical demonstration of our eschatological hope found in Christ. What is anticipated is not 'forced ecumenicalism' rather than the unity of Spirit and submission to biblical doctrine.[93] The emphasis is about prioritising the word over tradition, agreeing on core doctrines and interpretations, and praying for the unity of Church on this basis. A start point for instance is the certainty of His return, and restraint to fixing dates. Overall, eschatological study enriches the Pentecostal and Charismatic theology more deeply. I can now leave you with this question– do you look forward to the return of the Lord?

XXVI

ON SOCIAL JUSTICE AND A PENTECOST CHURCH RESPONSE

The principle being espoused in this section is that social concern and progressive action is a required response to injustice in community, by a believer, and the Church acting in tandem. The Church has grown through the centuries to recognise that social justice is a key element in its mission to reach a fallen world. David McIlroy, a theologian, has noted 'an increased sensitivity to the sufferings of the poor has led to a recognition of the importance of justice, and in particular the use of the law to enforce rights and entitlements, as a part of the

Church's mission.'[94] There is also however need for sensitivity to understand cultural tensions in society, in order to decipher willingness to receive support or give support. 'Race, ethnicity, and identity are critical in the cultural construction of meaning,' and it also raises issues of power and control, so cultural analysis is required.[95] Steve De Gruchy, has also suggested that exploring themes of social injustices also has a political and economic element to it, as there is reason to think that those that have systematically fought for and sought to maintain the foundations of racisms or economic syphoning of wealth, have benefits to gain.[96] Concern is raised by Gnana Robinson, but argues that the Church and body of Christ is to maintain its witness in the world by seeking for genuine conversion, as 'The object of true Christian mission should be change of hearts, not change of religion,'[97] as there is a sense that some become 'Christians' as being part of a social group not one that has been a transformative spiritual experience, which should be the case. As McIlroy had raised, Robinson also thinks the Church in her goals must bear the true 'face of Jesus, presented in the Bible,' which in Robinson's view had changed over time; because the God of the bible would concern for the poor, disadvantaged, and but also gave a spiritual message of good news.[98] The Church has a role to resist extended forms of priviledge from financial enslavement of the poor, in any form or in any place– Gruchy suggests the fight should be against 'globalised apartheid' and the 'Jim Crow' laws of the global economic order.[99] That is ensuring there is no institutional segregation where those who are less fortunate cannot have access to support systems. The interesting key is that the Church should be in the forefront of this global struggle, and not let those who wish to re-erect these mechanisms and opposed to the abolishment of injustices take a lead. 'Advocacy, as we have been reminded, is indeed an important part of the prophetic calling of the church,'[100] and that it is through the enabling of the Spirit of God that 'societal order and delivery and establishment' and the goal of 'global transformation' can be achieved.[101] As Walter Hollenweger, a Pentecostal Theologian and Professor of Intercultural Mission Theology, in his paper 'Ripe for Taking Risks?' had cautioned, when he acknowledged the problem often faced in society is that, 'It is not the fact that they are sinful men which is the main problem but that they are men with institutional power.'[102] Hence, the need for the 'power imbalance' to be addressed.[103]

i.   Pentecostalism Taking the Lead?

Allan Anderson has noted succinctly, that Pentecostalism have 'led the way on social issues like race, class, or gender equality.'[104] This is so especially when one considers that at the start of the 19th century the Church had slid-down to segregation and forceful sittings arrangements within Church meeting based on colour and ethnic differences. However, it was the revivalist efforts of the Pentecostal movement that changed that, and engendered calls for societal transformation. Following meetings where there had been baptism of the Spirit with evidence of tongues, led by William J. Seymour a Pentecostal preacher of the early 20th century, reports suggest there was racial equality and harmony, and many spiritual experiences in the assembly.[105] He faced some opposition from some ministers including one he worked under as his protégé, whose admonition on the matter he appears to have not taken after, as he was pro-equality, in support for people to gather together in worship irrespective of nationality– this later gained him notoriety. In essence, the Pentecostal Church's has led the way in society in terms of nature of public meetings, and in subsequent decades Christian meetings and public evangelical crusades would feature joint services, to the point Christians now also felt comfortable in engaging in interracial marriage without much persecution. Though these actions were decisive and public, some work had been started by previous movements,[106] whilst some of these practices continued. As Anderson would note, 'Pentecostal spirituality has the potential to transform oppressive structures.'[107] 'Pentecostal churches have helped establish and maintain autonomous organisations among the poor and provide opportunities for entrepreneurship and social mobility.'[108] For Pentecostals, the claim to be spirit-filled and empowered then, must also accompany evidence of a life that lives in 'righteous protest against the various-isms that perpetuate injustice in the world.'[109] The difficult question of what goodnews mean to the poor and marginalised must continue to be asked, 'a viable world Pentecostal theology for the twenty-first century cannot ignore this aspect of the biblical tradition.'[110] As Hollenweger would point out, Pentecostal traditions had long been to act against injustices, but there have been some within that have not lived up to its' ethos.[111]

ii.   Hermeneutical Argument

The Pentecostal response to social inequalities or injustices is anchored on scripture. It is a sense that injustice is an evil, and as a people to God we owe a responsibility to act against it, rather than be passive about rebuking such practices, benefit from, or abet efforts that seek its' entrenchment in society. 'Justice is always at the top of God's agenda.'[112] McIlroy shares the view that the relevance of justice is replete in scriptures, in the teachings of old testament prophets and also in the

Christ's doctrine and continued by the Apostles.[113] References would include, Isaiah 58, Psalm 146:7-9; Luke 4:19-21;10:25-37; Matthew 23:23, 25:40, 26:11; James 1:27; Proverbs 11:1; Job 34:12; Revelation 20:12-13; 2 Chronicles 19:7. From these scriptures, God is shown as detesting in strong terms injustices. In Isaiah, the Prophet is admonishing the Israelites, not only to perform spiritual activities as fasting and praying, but they had a responsibility to social justice in their community, and then God would in turn hear their prayers and rescue them- in verses 6-9,

'Is this not the fast that I have chosen:
To loose the bonds of wickedness,
To undo the heavy burdens,
To let the oppressed go free,
And that you break every yoke?
Is it not to share your bread with the hungry,
And that you bring to your house the poor who are cast out;
When you see the naked, that you cover him,
And not hide yourself from your own flesh?
Then your light shall break forth like the morning,
Your healing shall spring forth speedily,
And your righteousness shall go before you;
The glory of the Lord shall be your rear guard.

Then you shall call, and the Lord will answer;
You shall cry, and He will say, 'Here I *am.*'

'If you take away the yoke from your midst,
The pointing of the finger, and speaking
wickedness'

McIlroy argues that, not only the requirement for
social justice 'apparent' in the old testament, 'Any
adequate biblical theology of justice would have to
examine both the Exodus and the Torah for an
account of God's delivering purposes and guidelines
for a just society.'[114] The Torah is a reference to the
first five books in the old testament– *Pentateuch.* In
the old testament God is the one who avenges the
righteous and liberates the Jewish nation from
slavery, when they cried for help to Him.[115] Prophet
Isaiah's prophecy is a charge to let the oppress go
free, in the same way God had granted them justice
from their oppressors, and they were to take
responsibility as individuals and as a nation. 'The
force of the Prophets' message about justice is
inescapable, injustice has consequences, and the
ultimate consequences is the collapse of
civilisation.'[116] God warns, to avoid disaster. Jesus
Christ of Nazareth, in his earthly teachings
responded to the question of old testament's
commandments, on which was the greatest, in
Matthew 22:37-40 *kjv* , 'Jesus said unto him, Thou
shalt love the Lord thy God with all thy heart, and
with all thy soul, and with all thy mind. This is the
first and great commandment. And the second *is*

like unto it, Thou shalt love thy neighbour as thyself. On these two commandments hang all the law and the prophets.' Christ affirmed the need for social concern as one would for his own self. He also illustrated this principle in the good Samaritan parable.[117] He rebuked the leaders of His time who were marginal with the truth for personal aggrandisement.[118]

iii. Equality

Social justice would also mean tackling inequality within the Church's leadership system and in the social issues of our resident community. The Church has the moral responsibility to set the example by showing that it can effectively harnesses the human resources at its' hand. There is need for institutions within the Pentecostal movement to reappraise the level of effort it commits towards organisational integration, diversity and ethics of equality. As a failure to, could lead to a 'dilemma,'[119] or better encapsulated as series of neglect or injustices inadvertently geared at a group, either unintentionally or as a result of tardy practices and internal politics. Specifically, questions of institutional acceptance and equality of women to hold governing and ministerial role have arisen within the Church with Pentecostal and Evangelical ties,[120] and has been considered restrictive,[121] even though comparatively with other Christo-traditional denominations as the Orthodox and Catholic roots, are rather progressive. In fact, Pentecostals are considered 'pioneers' in this regard.[122] Structures would need to be in place that allows for the flourishing of both men and women ministries,[123] to aspirational levels, through reforms.[124] A spirit-filled person irrespective of gender should not have a cap placed on him or her– 'A believer's gifts and anointing should still today make a way for his or her ministry.'[125] The principle being if the Spirit releases why restrain? Un-naively, there are subjective concerns. The Church scripturally has a responsibility to uphold ministerial credible and Spirit-approved persons for offices, and not to operate to 'quench'[126] the Spirit as well as run the real risk of immaturity and causing offence because of insensitivity and ignorance of the Spirit's intent. If the Pentecostal Church would live up to its ideals and be effective, it would need to mobilise to support ministries based on competence, with a clear sign of the Spirit's affirmation, and as true to the word affirm such a person, man or woman– also, must mobilise to stand up for women's rights as may have been curtailed in some societies culturally, on issues of political office placements, gender pay gap, specific support for female employment leave based on anatomical considerations such as after birth, or on clear-cut restricted opportunity based on sex. Apart from the articulation of doctrine, the Church exist to show compassion and love.

iv.   Restoring the Church's Glory, Ecumenism, and Eschatological Hope

For the Evangelical movement, it has had to take the challenge of integrating into its Church practices the justice mission, and articulate its place in its theology.[127] One of the ways had been through the *Lausanne Covenant's Affirmation of Evangelism and Christian Social Responsibility* document that was drafted and produced as the sum total of agreement between a number of Christians and Evangelical Churches, which also included some with Pentecostal roots– to uphold the Church tenets of advocacy for those who were oppressed, or threatened to. Article 5 of the *Covenant* was to the effect– was a repentance of the Evangelical church for times it had thought of social concern as 'mutually exclusive' from evangelism, and neglected responsibility, though there is the consideration that reconciliation with others or social action is not reconciliation with God; but however affirmed the necessity to 'share his concern for justice and reconciliation throughout human society and for the liberation of men and women from every kind of oppression.'[128] It now seems there is a shift from the earlier teaching of 'evangelical individualism' which allowed some to ignore social concern, looking at the other side in guise that there was a sin problem to be addressed– other Christians and even some evangelicals within the camp criticised this heavily, because it allowed the corrupt to benefit, and caused discrimination, and also skewed proper teaching which meant human sin problem had to be addressed generally, but that other Christians also had a role to unitedly insist on social justice in manner in which activities were conducted where they lived[129]– as godly neighbours there is a responsibility to guide against repeated forms of inequalities that entrench generational disadvantages, for all.

Also, the efforts of non-Pentecostalist preachers, one of which– Martin Luther King, of the 20th century would be one of the strong voices speaking against racial and social inequalities of his day, and organising peaceful marches and talks in protests. Whilst the documented effort of Seymour, a Pentecostal preacher, at the start of the 20th century will usher in the call for racial harmony in the Church, by the mid-century Luther's call would be the need for racial harmony in America's society and across the world. By the end of the century, there had already been such a transformation, that a member of the black community and African-American, Barack Obama, with the support of those from within and other collective racial groups working in harmony, would be leading the country [as a legislator in the Senate] and as the nation's

President in the subsequent century, and championing the rights of all people utilising the breadth of the US's global leadership. The power of the Church cannot be underestimated when each individual, and the whole body, take steps towards achieving goals of social equality. Especially, in a globalised world, there is need for awareness of the 'interconnectedness' and 'transformation,'[130] as ideas are spreading and the possibility exists for movements to be reshaped and progressive change at grassroots. This is not to say, there would not be challenges, but leaps have been made against segregation, political rights, leadership, social economic advances– this will have to be deepened. And the Church of Christ has a role to carry on. The focus will be for continued expanding economic opportunities for all. This however, must not relegate the most important calling of saving souls, but neither neglect our responsibility to bodily care, and a worthy inheritance for the next generation. The Catholic missions, Orthodox Churches, and several other traditional churches have all contributed visibly a role in tackling social inequality in their communities over the centuries, often through the establishment of schools, hospitals, relief efforts etc, even though there are often some doctrinal disagreements with some other modern Churches, especially in relation to 'hierarchy' and the place of Christ as sole mediator to God. There is also the argument that it can be conceded that in some manner the Spirit had been involved ecumenically,[131] but should not restrain the progress towards theological soundness, perhaps of one of mercy over judgement in the Church. The journey may be 'gradual steps' not necessarily what is brought 'from non-existence to full existence in one leap.'[132] The willingness and fervour has to have been demonstrated. At the Christian ecumenical table, they could gather in affirmation of the Lordship of Christ, and also in support of fellow men in distress. As Dempster, points out the Church must stay relevant and be involved in social action, and not contemplate the imminent return of the Lord Jesus as a 'trump card' to carrying out this task,[133] but live with urgency.[134] It should rather spur on the efforts, as it is important to be 'occupying' and doing the work when He calls, and where Christ tarries the comfort of knowing a contribution has been made towards making lives better and a just reward that awaits the righteous by faith. There is need to live eschatologically, as those who look forward to the return of Christ when all things will be perfect without social inequalities or prejudices, under the Lordship of Christ, whilst also bearing the responsibility to live advancing the cause of justice until He returns. The glory of the Church in the 21st century, would be where it continually opens up to revisiting theological concerns to attain spiritual maturity, aim to grasp Christ's single truth for the Church, as God is not an author of confusion– however, the Church must not wait till when it's all agreeable on all issues to see reasons to support effort against inequality or poverty of the poor. Believers are also considering in modern times partnering with non-faith actors, which include NGOs to support humanitarian relief efforts.

Author's Biography Page

Israel Chukwuka Okunwaye, Dip.sc (Benin), LL. B (Benin), BL (Lagos), LLM (Birmingham), M.A (Birmingham)

Israel Chukwuka Okunwaye is a Christian Evangelist and minister of the gospel of Jesus Christ, called of God and with a heart to reach all people with the love that there is in Christ. For many years, now turning into decades he has been communicating this message of the Cross at the grassroots and also on several platforms with the fervour it demands, and with the tremendous spiritual grace the Lord supplies. He has written several works including these books, *Authentic Faith, The Heart of Passion,* and *Rethinking Leadership.* He believes that it is in the loving arms of God you will find all the answers you need. He is the founder of www.glyglobal.com, an online evangelistic network and outreach with free access to credible Christian faith resource and information, which has morphed into an instrumental tool in reaching many with the gospel across the nations, since the first launch many years ago. As a visionary, leader, and anointed speaker, he is graced to teach and minister the word with clarity, and prophetic unction. He also worked briefly as a human rights lawyer in Nigeria and is a staunch advocate for principles of social justice; and is concerned about the plight of the disadvantaged and affirm causes in aid. He believes that the call to Christian living should also drive social action.

He has been priviledged to lead a university campus Christian fellowship with Pentecostal roots, affiliated to Christ's Chosen Church of God Int'l, for some years as President, and thereafter as National President; and was involved in the University of Benin's Christian Community on Campus executive as the Public Relations Officer, a worthy cause of galvanising the body of Christ towards spiritual goals. Prior to this he has been involved with the Scripture Union locally, in encouraging young people and facilitating meetings. In Abuja– Nigeria, he led the work as Evangelism Coordinator under the auspices of the Nigeria Christian Corpers' Fellowship to mobilise efforts at reaching city dwellers and especially those in the rural areas with the gospel, and with practical relief support. Also, working alongside the team at an Elim Pentecostal Church in Selly Oak, Birmingham– UK as Evangelical worker led reaching out to the community and stirred the Church towards soul winning. As one with an evangelistic grace and zeal to see the frontiers for the gospel expand, he has been enabled to serve as Chaplain with CIGB UK [Churches and Industry Group Birmingham and Solihull] with a mission to minister to people at the workplace. He believes in the body of Christ being missional in the community where placed and has organised bible studies to explore and understand the Christian message in response to questions of faith; he continues to be at the forefront of teaching and conveying the word, through his resources, projects, and on speaking platforms. He identifies with the Evangelical Alliance UK as a member. Evangelist Israel, hold in affirmation the foundational doctrines of faith along with fellow believers, and the Apostles' Creed. He has attended the International Bible Institute of London [IBIOL], Kensington Temple, London, studying the course on Apologetics, and also a Church based ministry training programme, Midlands Ministry Training Course [MMTC], at the Midlands Gospel Partnership, Birmingham.

He is a M.A graduate of the School of Philosophy, Theology and Religion, of University of Birmingham, and has an LLM from the Birmingham Law School. He has also received a BL from the Nigeria Law School, Lagos, after completing his bachelor's degree with the University of Benin.

For further information on ministry update and contact– www.israelokunwaye.com.

BIBLIOGRAPHY

Allan Anderson, 'A 'Time to Share Love': Global Pentecostalism and the Social Ministry of David Yonggi Cho' (2012) 21 *Journal of Pentecostal Theology* 152-167

Amos Young, 'Justice Deprived, Justice Demanded: Afropentecostalisms and the Task of World Pentecostal Theology Today' (2006) 1 *Journal of Pentecostal Theology* 127-147

Cecil M. Robeck, 'Pentecostals and Social Ethics' (1987) *Pneuma: The Journal of the Society for Pentecostal Studies* 103-107

Amos Young, 'Pentecostalism and the Political- Trajectories in its Second Century' (2010) 32 *Pneuma* 333-336

Amy Orr-ewing, *Why trust the bible? Answers to 10 tough questions* (Intervarsity Press England, 2005)

Andrew Davis, 'The Spirit of Freedom: Pentecostals, the Bible and Social Justice' (2011) 31(1) *Journal of the European Pentecostal Theological Association* 53-64

Anton Houtepen, 'Apocalyptics and the Kingdom of God: Christian Eschatology and the 'pursuit of the millennium' (1999) 28(4) *Exchange* 290

Calvin Smith, 'Revolutionaries and Revivalists: Pentecostal Eschatology, Politics and Nicaraguan Revolution' (2008) 30 *Pneuma* 55

Caroline Jeannerat, 'Of Lizards, Misfortune and Deliverance: Pentecostal Soteriology in the Life of a Migrant' (2009) *African Studies* 251

Claire Randall, 'The Importance of the Pentecostal and Holiness Churches in the
Ecumenical Movement' (1986) *Pneuma: The Journal of the Society for Pentecostal Studies* 50-60

Cornelius Tacitus, Annals: Book 15, ed. By N. Miller (Bristol, Bristol Classical Press Latin Texts, 1998)

Curtis Evans, 'White Evangelical Protestant Responses to the Civil Rights Movement' (2009) 102(2) *Harvard Theological Review* 245-273

Dale Coutler, 'Delivered by the power of God: towards a Pentecostal understanding on salvation' (2008) 10(4) *International Journal of Systematic Theology* 1468

Dale M. Coulter, 'Pentecostal Visions of the end: Eschatology, Ecclesiology and the Fascination of the Left Behind Series' (2015) *Journal of Pentecostal Theology* 81

Dan Graves, 'Charlotte Elliott Faced God with One Plea' July 2007 *Christianity* < http://www.christianity.com/church/church-history/timeline/1801-1900/charlotte-elliott-faced-god-with-one-plea-11630559.html>

Daniel Castelo, Tarrying on the Lord: Affections, Virtues and Theological Ethics in Pentecostal Perspectives (2004) 13(1) *Journal of Pentecostal Theology* 31

David Ford, 'Jesus Christ, the Wisdom of God (1)' in David Ford and Graham Stanton (Edrs) *Reading Texts, Seeking Wisdom* (SCM Press, 2003)

David McIlroy, 'The Mission of Justice' (2011) 28(3) *Transformation* 182-194

David Neff, 'Christian History: 'How Great thou Art' & the 100-year-old Bass, The story of George Beverly Shea's Signature Tune' April 17, 2013 *Christianity Today* < http://www.christianitytoday.com/ct/2013/april-web-only/how-great-thou-art-100-year-old-bass.html>

Diane Severance, 'William Williams, Welsh Evangelist' June 2007 *Christianity* < http://www.christianity.com/church/church-history/timeline/1701-1800/william-williams-welsh-evangelist-11630199.html>; Rupert Christiansen, 'Guide me o thou Great Jehovah' <

http://www.telegraph.co.uk/culture/music/3668065/The-story-behind-the-hymn.html> .

Douglas J. Moo, 'Jesus and the Authority of the Mosaic Law' in Craig A. Evans and Stanley E. Porter (Eds) The Historical Jesus (Sheffield Academic Press, 1995)

Edith Blumhofer, 'Focus: Women and Pentecostalism' (1995) 17(1) *The Journal of the Society for Pentecostal Studies* 19

Ferdinand Sutterlüty, 'The Role of Religious Ideas: Christian Interpretations of Social Inequalities' (2016) *Critical Sociology* 33

Geoffrey Wainwright, 'The One Hope of Your Calling? The Ecumenical and Pentecostal Movements after a Century' (2003) 25(1) *Pneuma: The Journal of the Society for Pentecostal Studies* 7-28

Glenn Balfour, 'Pentecostal Eschatology Revisited' (2011) 31(2) *European Pentecostal Theological Association* 127

Gnana Robinson, "Mission in Christ's Way': The Way of Which Christ?' (2006) 35(3) *Exchange* 270-277, 272.

Hymntime, 'Guide me o thou Great Jehovah' http://www.hymntime.com/tch/htm/g/u/i/guideme.htm.

Hymntime, 'How Great Thou Art,' < http://www.hymntime.com/tch/htm/h/o/w/how_great_T hou_art.htm>

Hymntime, 'Just as I am without one plea' http://www.hymntime.com/tch/htm/j/u/s/justasam.htm

Jesse A. Hoover, "Thy Daughters Shall Prophesy': The Assemblies of God, Inerrancy, and the Question of Clergywomen' (2012) 21 *Journal of Pentecostal Theology* 221-239

Joe Creech, 'Visions of Glory: The Place of the Azusa Street Revival in Pentecostal History' (1996) 65(3) *Church History* 405-424

Julie Ma, 'Eschatology and Mission: Living the 'Last Days' Today' (2009) 26(3) *Transformation* 194

Kenneth Archer, 'The Fivefold Gospel and the Mission of the Church: Ecclesiastical Implications and Opportunities' in John Thomas (ed.), *Toward a Pentecostal Ecclessiology: The Church and the Fivefold Gospel* (2010, CPT Tennessee) 5

Margaret Poloma, 'Charisma, Institutionalization and Social Change' (1995) 17 *Pneuma* 245

Margaret Poloma, 'Women in the Ministry: The Dilemma of Mixed Motivation' in *The Assemblies of God at the Crossroads: Charisma and Institutional Dilemmas* (University of Tennessee Press, Knoxville 1989) 103

Mark Snoeberger, 'Tongues: Are they for Today' (2009) 21(3) *Detroit Baptist Seminary Journal* 4

Matt Slick, 'What is Dispensationalism?' Christian Apologetics and Research Ministry < https://carm.org/dispensationalism>

Matthew Thompson, 'Eschatology as Soteriology: The Cosmic Full Gospel' in Peter Althouse, Robby Waddell (eds) *Perspectives in Pentecostal Eschatologies: World without End* (Jemes Clarke & co, 2010) 203

Michael Wilkinson, 'What's 'Global' about Global Pentecostalism' (2008) 17 *Journal of Pentecostal Theology* 96-109

Miroslav Volf, 'Materiality of Salvation: An investigation in the soteriologies of liberation and Pentecostal theology' (1989) 26(3) *Journal of Ecumenical Studies* 447

Murray Dempster, 'Christian Social Concern in Pentecostal Perspective: Reformulating Pentecostal Eschatology' (1993) 2 *Journal of Pentecostal Theology* 51

Murray Dempster, 'Christian Social Concern in Pentecostal Perspective: Reformulating Pentecostal Eschatology' (1993) 2 *Journal of Pentecostal Theology* 51

N.T. Wright, *Scripture and the Authority of God* (SPCK 2005)

Peter Althouse, 'The Landscape of Pentecostal and Charismatic Eschatology' in Peter Althouse, Robby Waddell (eds) *Perspectives in Pentecostal Eschatologies: World without End* (Jemes Clarke & co, 2010) 15

Peter Althouse and Robby Waddell, 'Pentecostalism, Cultural Analysis, and the Hermeneutics of Culture' (2015) 37 *Pneuma* 313-316

Peter D. Hocken, 'Liturgy and Eschatology in a Pentecostal-Charismatic Ecumenism' (2012) Ecumenical Studies Group, in 41st Annual Meeting of the Society for Pentecostal Studies 1

Peter D. Hocken, 'Liturgy and Eschatology in a Pentecostal-Charismatic Ecumenism' 4
Robert C. Crosby, 'A New Kind of Pentecostal' *Christianity Today* August 3, 2011 < http://www.christianitytoday.com/ct/2011/august/newkin dpentecostal.html>

Robert L. Webb, 'The Historical Enterprise and Historical Jesus Research' in Darrell L. Bock and Robert L. Webb (Eds), *Key Events in the Life of Historical Jesus: A Collaborative Exploration of Context and Coherence* (Eerdmans Publishing, Cambridge 2009)

Ruth Caroline Christiansen, 'How Great Thou Art, the Story: Composer Carl Boberg Writes How Great Thou Art' *Share Faith* < http://www.sharefaith.com/guide/Christian-Music/hymns-the-songs-and-the-stories/how-great-thou-art-the-story.html>.

Ruth Caroline Christiansen, 'Just as I am, the Song and the Story' *Share faith* < http://www.sharefaith.com/guide/Christian-Music/hymns-the-songs-and-the-stories/just-as-i-am,-the-song-and-the-story.html>

Steve De Gruchy, 'Religion and Racism: Struggle around Segregation, 'Jim Crow' and Apartheid' in Hugh Mcleod (ed), World Christianities c.1914–c.2000 (Cambridge University Press) 385

Steven Studebaker, 'Pentecostal Soteriology and Pneumatology' (2003) 11(2) *Journal of Pentecostal Theology* 248

The General Presbytery of the Assemblies of God USA, 'The Role of Women in Ministry,' 2010 statement.

The Lausanne Movement, 'The Lausanne Covenant' https://www.lausanne.org/content/covenant/lausanne-covenant

Thomas O'Dea, 'Five Dilemmas in the Institutionalization of Religion' (1961) 1 *Journal for the Scientific study of Religion* 30-39

Tim Grass, 'The Ecumenical Movement' (2008) *Modern Church History* 318-335

Tim LaHaye, Left Behind, (Carol Stream, IL: Tyndale House, 1995-2007) series

Veli-Matti Kärkäinen, 'Are Pentecostals Oblivious to Social Justice? Theological and Ecumenical Perspectives?' (2001) XXIX(4) *Missiology: An International Review* 417

Walter Hollenweger, 'Ripe for Taking Risks?' (1996) 18(1) *Pneuma: The Journal of the Society for Pentecostal Studies* 107-112

Walter Hollenweger, 'The Critical Tradition of Pentecostalism' (1992) 1 *Journal of Pentecostal Theology* 7-17

William A. Clark, 'Clarifying the Spiritual Value of Forests and their Role in Sustainable Forest Management' (2011) 5(1) *Journal for the Study of Religion, Nature and Culture* 29-30

William Faupel, 'The Function of 'Models' in the Interpretation of Pentecostal Thought' (1980) *Pnuema: The Journal of the Society for Pentecostal Studies* 51

William G. Rusch, 'The Theology of the Holy Spirit and the Pentecostal Churches in the Ecumenical Movement' (1986) *Pneuma: The Journal of the Society for Pentecostal Studies* 17-30

William L. Craig, *Reasonable Faith* (Crossway, 2008)

Notes

¹ William L. Craig, *Reasonable Faith* (Crossway, 2008) 416; Robert L. Webb, 'The Historical Enterprise and Historical Jesus Research' in Darrell L. Bock and Robert L. Webb (Eds), *Key Events in the Life of Historical Jesus: A Collaborative Exploration of Context and Coherence* (Eerdmans Publishing, Cambridge 2009) 9, 931- explores in depth historicity and research methods on this theological area; he suggests reference can be made to the synoptic gospels evidences, ancient Jewish writings and credible secular sources from the ancient Mediterranean times to galvanise data. However, whoever the historian is they too must be open to discovery- 'Not only does the historian's awareness and knowledge develop, it is also possible that the historian's perspective and values are altered as well. This should not only be allowed, it should be encouraged, for history should contribute to one's growth and development as a human being.' Pg. 52; Douglas J. Moo, 'Jesus and the Authority of the Mosaic Law' in Craig A. Evans and Stanley E. Porter (Eds) The Historical Jesus (Sheffield Academic Press, 1995) 83.

² Amy Orr-ewing, *Why trust the bible? Answers to 10 tough questions* (Intervarsity Press England, 2005) 128, P. 38.

³ Amy Orr-Ewing, 'Why Trust the Bible?' 39.

⁴ Amy Orr-Ewing, 'Why Trust the Bible?' 40.

⁵ Ibid, pg 55.

[6] Cornelius Tacitus, Annals: Book 15, ed. By N. Miller (Bristol, Bristol Classical Press Latin Texts, 1998, 44).

[7] Apart from navigating the historical contours of faith the inquirer must seek to consider what this new discovery of the historical Jesus, now means- David Ford, 'Jesus Christ, the Wisdom of God (1)' in David Ford and Graham Stanton (Edrs) *Reading Texts, Seeking Wisdom* (SCM press, 2003) 4-21, 19. N.T. Wright, *Scripture and the Authority of God* (SPCK 2005).

[8] Kenneth Archer, 'The Fivefold Gospel and the Mission of the Church: Ecclesiastical Implications and Opportunities' in John Thomas (ed.), *Toward a Pentecostal Ecclessiology: The Church and the Fivefold Gospel* (2010, CPT Tennessee) 5.

[9] Kenneth Archer, 'The Fivefold Gospel and the Mission of the Church.'

[10] Dale Coutler, 'Delivered by the power of God: towards a Pentecostal understanding on salvation' (2008) 10(4) *International Journal of Systematic Theology* 1468

[11] Steven Studebaker, 'Pentecostal Soteriology and Pneumatology' (2003) 11(2) *Journal of Pentecostal Theology* 248.

[12] Caroline Jeannerat, 'Of Lizards, Misfortune and Deliverance: Pentecostal Soteriology in the Life of a Migrant' (2009) African Studies 251

[13] 1 John 5:12

[14] Proverbs 21:31

[15] Miroslav Volf, 'Materiality of Salvation: An investigation in the soteriologies of liberation and Pentecostal theology' (1989) 26(3) *Journal of Ecumenical Studies* 447.

[16] Caroline Jeannerat, 'Of Lizards, Misfortune and Deliverance' 253.

[17] William Faupel, 'The Function of 'Models' in the Interpretation of Pentecostal Thought' (1980) Pnuema: The Journal of the Society for Pentecostal Studies 51.

[18] I Corinthians 13:3.

[19] Matthew 6:33.

[20] Hymntime, 'How Great Thou Art,' < http://www.hymntime.com/tch/htm/h/o/w/how_great_Thou_art.htm>

[21] Ruth Caroline Christiansen, 'How Great Thou Art, the Story: Composer Carl Boberg Writes How Great Thou Art' *Share Faith* < http://www.sharefaith.com/guide/Christian-Music/hymns-the-songs-and-the-stories/how-great-thou-art-the-story.html>.

[22] David Neff, 'Christian History: 'How Great thou Art' & the 100-year-old Bass, The story of George Beverly Shea's Signature Tune' April 17, 2013 *Christianity Today* < http://www.christianitytoday.com/ct/2013/april-web-only/how-great-thou-art-100-year-old-bass.html>

[23] William A. Clark, 'Clarifying the Spiritual Value of Forests and their Role in Sustainable Forest Management' (2011) 5(1) *Journal for the Study of Religion, Nature and Culture* 29-30.

[24] Hymntime, 'How Great Thou Art.'

[25] Hymntime, 'Just as I am without one plea' <http://www.hymntime.com/tch/htm/j/u/s/justasam.htm>

[26] Dan Graves, 'Charlotte Elliott Faced God with One Plea' July 2007 *Christianity* < http://www.christianity.com/church/church-history/timeline/1801-1900/charlotte-elliott-faced-god-with-one-plea-11630559.html>

[27] Ruth Caroline Christiansen, 'Just as I am, the Song and the Story' *Share faith* < http://www.sharefaith.com/guide/Christian-Music/hymns-the-songs-and-the-stories/just-as-i-am,-the-song-and-the-story.html>.

[28] Hymntime, 'Just as I am without one plea.'

[29] Diane Severance, 'William Williams, Welsh Evangelist' June 2007 *Christianity* < http://www.christianity.com/church/church-history/timeline/1701-1800/william-williams-welsh-evangelist-11630199.html>; Rupert Christiansen, 'Guide me o thou Great Jehovah' < http://www.telegraph.co.uk/culture/music/3668065/The-story-behind-the-hymn.html> .

[30] Hymntime, 'Guide me o thou Great Jehovah' http://www.hymntime.com/tch/htm/g/u/i/guideme.htm.

[31] Kenneth Archer, 'The Fivefold Gospel and the Mission of the Church: Ecclesiastical Implications and Opportunities' in John

Thomas (ed.), *Toward a Pentecostal Ecclessiology: The Church and the Fivefold Gospel* (2010, CPT Tennessee) 5.
[32] Kenneth Archer, 'The Fivefold Gospel and the Mission of the Church.'
[33] *Written by Israel Okunwaye*
[34] *Written by Israel Okunwaye*
[35] Peter D. Hocken, 'Liturgy and Eschatology in a Pentecostal-Charismatic Ecumenism' (2012) Ecumenical Studies Group, in 41st Annual Meeting of the Society for Pentecostal Studies 1.
[36] Peter D. Hocken, 'Liturgy and Eschatology in a Pentecostal-Charismatic Ecumenism' 4
[37] Calvin Smith, 'Revolutionaries and Revivalists: Pentecostal Eschatology, Politics and Nicaraguan Revolution' (2008) 30 *Pneuma* 55, 57
[38] Glenn Balfour, 'Pentecostal Eschatology Revisited' (2011) 31(2) European Pentecostal Theological Association 127
[39] Glenn Balfour, 'Pentecostal Eschatology' 128.
[40] Mark Snoeberger, 'Tongues: Are they for Today' (2009) 21(3) Detroit Baptist Seminary Journal 4.
[41] Glenn Balfour, 'Pentecostal Eschatology' 129.
[42] Glenn Balfour, 'Pentecostal Eschatology' 129.
[43] Calvin Smith, 'Revolutionaries and Revivalists' 59.
[44] 1 Timothy 4.
[45] Glenn Balfour, 'Pentecostal Eschatology' 129.
[46] Glenn Balfour, 'Pentecostal Eschatology' 130.
[47] Glenn Balfour, 'Pentecostal Eschatology' 131,132.
[48] Romans 11.
[49] Dale M. Coulter, 'Pentecostal Visions of the end: Eschatology, Ecclesiology and the Fascination of the Left Behind Series' (2015) Journal of Pentecostal Theology 81, 82.
[50] Dale M. Coulter, 'Pentecostal Visions of the end' 84.
[51] Matt Slick, 'What is Dispensationalism?' Christian Apologetics and Research Ministry < https://carm.org/dispensationalism>
[52] Calvin Smith, 'Revolutionaries and Revivalists' 58.
[53] Peter Althouse, 'The Landscape of Pentecostal and Charismatic Eschatology' in Peter Althouse, Robby Waddell (eds) *Perspectives in Pentecostal Eschatologies: World without End* (Jemes Clarke & co, 2010) 15

[54] Peter Althouse, 'The Landscape of Pentecostal and Charismatic Eschatology' 1.

[55] Peter Althouse, 'The Landscape of Pentecostal and Charismatic Eschatology' 2.

[56] Tim LaHaye, Left Behind, (Carol Stream, IL: Tyndale House, 1995-2007) series

[57] Peter Althouse, 'The Landscape of Pentecostal and Charismatic Eschatology' 2.

[58] Peter Althouse, 'The Landscape of Pentecostal and Charismatic Eschatology' 3.

[59] Matthew 24.

[60] 1 Peter 4:11; Galatians 1:8-9.

[61] Peter Althouse, 'The Landscape of Pentecostal and Charismatic Eschatology' 3.

[62] Peter Althouse, 'The Landscape of Pentecostal and Charismatic Eschatology' 4.

[63] Peter Althouse, 'The Landscape of Pentecostal and Charismatic Eschatology' 4.

[64] Anton Houtepen, 'Apocalyptics and the Kingdom of God: Christian Eschatology and the 'pursuit of the millennium' (1999) 28(4) *Exchange* 290, 294

[65] Peter Althouse, 'The Landscape of Pentecostal and Charismatic Eschatology' 4.

[66] Anton Houtepen, 'Apocalyptics and the Kingdom of God' 292, 293.

[67] Murray Dempster, 'Christian Social Concern in Pentecostal Perspective: Reformulating Pentecostal Eschatology' (1993) 2 *Journal of Pentecostal Theology* 51, 59. There is a strong sense that being 'salt' means adding flavour and preservation to the earth, not losing value rather continually being relevant to the kingdom of God whilst on earth, so the work of God prospers here on earth as we as believers reach souls for Christ.

[68] Murray Dempster, 'Christian Social Concern in Pentecostal Perspective' 59.

[69] Murray Dempster, 'Christian Social Concern in Pentecostal Perspective' 60.

[70] Murray Dempster, 'Christian Social Concern in Pentecostal Perspective' 60.

71 Murray Dempster, 'Christian Social Concern in Pentecostal Perspective' 60.

72 Robert C. Crosby, 'A New Kind of Pentecostal' *Christianity Today* August 3, 2011 < http://www.christianitytoday.com/ct/2011/august/newkindpentecos tal.html>.

73 Robert Crosby, 'A New Kind of Pentecostal' 3.

74 Philippians 1:22-24; John 14:1-3.

75 Peter Althouse, 'The Landscape of Pentecostal and Charismatic Eschatology' 12.

76 Luke 13:18-20, 17:21, Matthew 6:10

77 Peter Althouse, 'The Landscape of Pentecostal and Charismatic Eschatology' 13.

78 Matthew Thompson, 'Eschatology as Soteriology: The Cosmic Full Gospel' in Peter Althouse, Robby Waddell (eds) *Perspectives in Pentecostal Eschatologies: World without End* (Jemes Clarke & co, 2010)203

79 Matthew Thompson, 'Eschatology as Soteriology' 203.

80 Matthew Thompson, 'Eschatology as Soteriology' 203.

81 Matthew Thompson, 'Eschatology as Soteriology' 203.

82 Julie Ma, 'Eschatology and Mission: Living the 'Last Days' Today' (2009) 26(3) *Transformation* 194

83 Julie Ma, 'Eschatology and Mission' 193

84 Julie Ma, 'Eschatology and Mission' 190.

85 Calvin Smith, 'Revolutionaries and Revivalists' 55, 66-68.

86 Calvin Smith, 'Revolutionaries and Revivalists' 68.

87 Calvin Smith, 'Revolutionaries and Revivalists' 77.

88 Romans 12:12, James 1:2-4.

89 Daniel Castelo, Tarrying on the Lord: Affections, Virtues and Theological Ethics in Pentecostal Perspectives (2004) 13(1) *Journal of Pentecostal Theology* 31.

90 Dale M. Coulter, 'Pentecostal Visions of the end: Eschatology, Ecclesiology and the Fascination of the Left Behind Series' (2015) *Journal of Pentecostal Theology* 81, 96

91 Julie Ma, 'Eschatology and Mission' 186.

92 Julie Ma, 'Eschatology and Mission' 187.

93 Dale Coulter, 'Pentecostal Visions of the end' 94.

[94] David Mcllroy, 'The Mission of Justice' (2011) 28(3) *Transformation* 182-194, 183.

[95] Peter Althouse and Robby Waddell, 'Pentecostalism, Cultural Analysis, and the Hermeneutics of Culture' (2015) 37 *Pneuma* 313-316, 314, 315.

[96] Steve De Gruchy, 'Religion and Racism: Struggle around Segregation, 'Jim Crow' and Apartheid' in Hugh Mcleod (ed), World Christianities c.1914–c.2000 (Cambridge University Press) 385.

[97] Gnana Robinson, "Mission in Christ's Way': The Way of Which Christ?' (2006) 35(3) *Exchange* 270-277, 272.

[98] Gnana Robinson, Mission in Christ's Way, 273.

[99] Steve De Gruchy, Religion and Racism, 400.

[100] Andrew Davis, 'The Spirit of Freedom: Pentecostals, the Bible and Social Justice' (2011) 31(1) *Journal of the European Pentecostal Theological Association* 53-64, 56.

[101] Andrew Davis, The Spirit of Freedom, 58.

[102] Walter Hollenweger, 'Ripe for Taking Risks?' (1996) 18(1) *Pneuma: The Journal of the Society for Pentecostal Studies* 107-112, 110.

[103] Walter Hollenweger, Ripe for Taking Risks? 111.

[104] Allan Anderson, 'A 'Time to Share Love': Global Pentecostalism and the Social Ministry of David Yonggi Cho' (2012) 21 *Journal of Pentecostal Theology* 152-167, 152.

[105] Joe Creech, 'Visions of Glory: The Place of the Azusa Street Revival in Pentecostal History' (1996) 65(3) *Church History* 405-424, 410.

[106] Allan Anderson, A 'Time to Share Love, 154.

[107] Allan Anderson, A 'Time to Share Love, 156.

[108] Wolfgang Vondey, Impact of Culture and Social Justice, 205.

[109] Amos Young, 'Pentecostalism and the Political- Trajectories in its Second Century' (2010) 32 *Pneuma* 333-336, 336.

[110] Amos Young, 'Justice Deprived, Justice Demanded: Afropentecostalisms and the Task of World Pentecostal Theology Today' (2006) 1 Journal of Pentecostal Theology 127-147, 134; Cecil M. Robeck, 'Pentecostals and Social Ethics' (1987) *Pneuma: The Journal of the Society for Pentecostal Studies* 103-107.

[111] Walter Hollenweger, 'The Critical Tradition of Pentecostalism' (1992) 1 *Journal of Pentecostal Theology* 7-17; Veli-Matti Kärkäinen, 'Are Pentecostals Oblivious to Social Justice? Theological and

Ecumenical Perspectives?' (2001) XXIX(4) *Missiology: An International Review* 417, argues that though the movement led the efforts in tackling the injustice of racism, also within its movement, concerns gradually emerged. He suggests the need to pay attention to tackle these concerns.

[112] David Mcllroy, The Mission of Justice, 184.

[113] David Mcllroy, The Mission of Justice, 183.

[114] David Mcllroy, The Mission of Justice, 183.

[115] Exodus 3:9-10; The question has been raised whether the *Exodus* experience, can form a 'religious idea' that informs social action or 'liberation' movements or political policies, that justify social inequalities? Ferdinand Sutterlüty, 'The Role of Religious Ideas: Christian Interpretations of Social Inequalities' (2016) *Critical Sociology* 33. What is important to consider is the interpretation given to these scenarios, whether they consider the responsibilities of those involved in the dialectics- the parties in the story, the right to 'ownership' or rights, juxtaposition of themes of oppression and redemption on the other hand, power imbalance, entitlement to restitution over a period of time, divine intervention etc Also the religious idea has to be one from scripture, and read in context and alongside other scriptures on the subject matter.

[116] David Mcllroy, The Mission of Justice, 185.

[117] Luke 10:25-37.

[118] Matthew 23:23 *nkjv*- "Woe to you, scribes and Pharisees, hypocrites! For you pay tithe of mint and anise and cummin, and have neglected the weightier *matters* of the law: justice and mercy and faith. These you ought to have done, without leaving the others undone.'

[119] Thomas O'Dea, 'Five Dilemmas in the Institutionalization of Religion' (1961) 1 *Journal for the Scientific study of Religion* 30-39.

[120] Edith Blumhofer, 'Focus: Women and Pentecostalism' (1995) 17(1) *The Journal of the Society for Pentecostal Studies* 19.

[121] Margaret Poloma, 'Women in the Ministry: The Dilemma of Mixed Motivation' in *The Assemblies of God at the Crossroads: Charisma and Institutional Dilemmas* (University of Tennessee Press, Knoxville 1989) 103.

[122] Claire Randall, 'The Importance of the Pentecostal and Holiness Churches in the Ecumenical Movement' (1986) *Pneuma: The Journal of the Society for Pentecostal Studies* 50-60, 57.

[123] Margaret Poloma, 'Charisma, Institutionalization and Social Change' (1995) 17 *Pneuma* 245.

[124] Jesse A. Hoover, "'Thy Daughters Shall Prophesy': The Assemblies of God, Inerrancy, and the Question of Clergywomen' (2012) 21 *Journal of Pentecostal Theology* 221-239.

[125] The General Presbytery of the Assemblies of God USA, 'The Role of Women in Ministry,' 2010 statement.

[126] 1 Thessalonians 5:19-22

[127] David McIlroy, The Mission of Justice, 188.

[128] The Lausanne Movement, 'The Lausanne Covenant' https://www.lausanne.org/content/covenant/lausanne-covenant accessed August 5, 2017.

[129] Curtis Evans, 'White Evangelical Protestant Responses to the Civil Rights Movement' (2009) 102(2) *Harvard Theological Review* 245-273.

[130] Michael Wilkinson, 'What's 'Global' about Global Pentecostalism' (2008) 17 *Journal of Pentecostal Theology* 96-109,103.

[131] William G. Rusch, 'The Theology of the Holy Spirit and the Pentecostal Churches in the Ecumenical Movement' (1986) *Pneuma: The Journal of the Society for Pentecostal Studies* 17-30; Geoffrey Wainwright, 'The One Hope of Your Calling? The Ecumenical and Pentecostal Movements after a Century' (2003) 25(1) *Pneuma: The Journal of the Society for Pentecostal Studies* 7-28.

[132] Tim Grass, 'The Ecumenical Movement' (2008) *Modern Church History* 318-335.

[133] Murray Dempster, 'Christian Social Concern in Pentecostal Perspective: Reformulating Pentecostal Eschatology' (1993) 2 *Journal of Pentecostal Theology* 51, 59.

[134] Julie Ma, 'Eschatology and Mission: Living the 'Last Days' Today' (2009) 26(3) *Transformation* 194.

www.ingramcontent.com/pod-product-compliance
Lightning Source LLC
Chambersburg PA
CBHW030924090426
42737CB00007B/314